COMPOSING
QUALITATIVE
RESEARCH

SECOND EDITION

COMPOSING QUALITATIVE RESEARCH

Karen Golden-Biddle
University of Alberta, Canada

Karen Locke
College of William and Mary

SAGE Publications
Thousand Oaks ■ London ■ New Delhi

For information:

Sage Publications, Inc.
2455 Teller Road
Thousand Oaks, California 91320
E-mail: order@sagepub.com

Sage Publications Ltd.
1 Oliver's Yard
55 City Road
London EC1Y 1SP
United Kingdom

Sage Publications India Pvt. Ltd.
B-42, Panchsheel Enclave
Post Box 4109
New Delhi 110 017 India

Printed in the United States of America.

Library of Congress Cataloging-in-Publication Data

Golden-Biddle, Karen.
Composing qualitative research / Karen Golden-Biddle, Karen
Locke.— 2nd ed.
    p. cm.
Includes bibliographical references and index.
ISBN 1-4129-0561-3 (pbk.)
  1. Technical writing. I. Locke, Karen II. Title.
T11.G63 2007
808′.0666—dc22

                                  2006006478

This book is printed on acid-free paper.

06   07   08   09   10   10 9 8 7 6 5 4 3 2 1

Acquiring Editor:	Lisa Cuevas Shaw
Editorial Assistant:	Karen Gia Wong
Project Editor:	Astrid Virding
Copyeditor:	Kristin Bergstad
Typesetter:	C&M Digitals (P) Ltd.
Indexer:	Kathy Paparchontis
Cover Designer:	Glenn Vogel

Win a FREE iPod®!

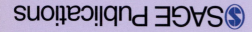

5 Easy Steps to Win $500!

STEP 1) Please Sign-in or Create a New Account
(login or enter your e-mail address)

STEP 2) Create Account
(Be sure to choose a role!)

STEP 3) Add Institution
(and your department)

STEP 4) Add or Edit Your Course
(Add multiple courses so we can send you
free exam copies for all your needs)

STEP 5) Your Account is Complete

Congratulations, you are now entered to win one of three
$500 American Express© Gift Cards*

⑤SAGE Publications

*Contest expires September 30th, 2006. Complete contest rules available at
www.sagepublications.com/profile

CONTENTS

Acknowledgments   vii

Introduction   1

     Writing About Writing   2

     Writing Our Fieldwork   4

     Focus on "Theorized Storyline"   5

     Organization of Chapters   6

1. The Style and Practice of Our Academic Writing   9

     The Predominant Style of Academic Writing: Unadorned
        and Disembodied   10

     Experiencing the Practice of Academic Writing   11

         Write It Up, But *What* Do We Write?   13

         Write It Up, But *For Whom* Do We Write?   14

         Write It Up, But *Under What Terms* Will Our Writing Be
         Granted a Disciplinary Audience?   17

     The Style and Practice of Academic Writing: Interested
        and Persuasive Discourse   17

     Our Writing Task   23

2. Crafting a Theorized Storyline   25

     Establishing Theorized Storylines   26

     Move 1: Articulate Study Significance   27

     Move 2: Situate Study in Literature   31

         Synthesized Coherence   33

         Progressive Coherence   34

         Noncoherence   36

     Move 3: Problematize Literature to Make Space
        for Study to Contribute   37

         Incomplete   38

Inadequate 39

Incommensurate 41

Move 4: Foreshadow How the Present Study
Addresses Problematization 44

3. Developing the Theorized Storyline **47**

Compelling Beginnings 48

Novel Use of Methodology Sections 51

Data–Theory Coupling 52

Telling, Showing, and Telling 53

Minimal Telling, Showing, Telling, More General Telling 55

Storylines With Field and Theory Complications 57

4. Characterizing the Storyteller **61**

Storyteller in the Guise of Institutional and Human Scientist 63

Institutional and Human Storyteller in Relationship to
the Studied 68

Institutional and Human Portrayals as Technically
Competent Storyteller 71

Institutional and Human Scientist as Field-Knowledgeable
Storyteller 76

5. Re-Writing the Story **81**

Re-Writing the Manuscript Prior to Journal Review 83

Re-Writing the Manuscript During the Journal Review Process 86

Engaging and Re-Writing the Field Story and
What It Is About 87

Re-Writing the Articulated Theorized Storylines 91

How Authors Engage Reviewer Suggestions for
Re-Writing the Manuscript 100

Reflections on the Re-Written Manuscripts 108

Conclusion 110

Concluding Comments **113**

Writing and Re-Writing 114

Sharing 115

Reading 115

References **117**

Index **127**

About the Authors **135**

ACKNOWLEDGMENTS

———•◦•———

We would like to thank the numerous colleagues who shared their comments about the original version of this book, including what was most useful and what they wanted to see expanded in the second edition. We also extend heartfelt thanks to the colleagues who opened up their review processes for us to write about in Chapter 5.

Sage Publications thanks the following reviewers: Julie Hartley, Brigham Young University; Joseph A. Kotarba, University of Houston; S. Kim MacGregor, Louisiana State University; and Demetra Smith Nightingale, Johns Hopkins University, Institute for Policy Studies.

INTRODUCTION

I n introducing the first edition of this book, we noted that we, like many other researchers we know who utilize qualitative data, have grappled with how to transform our fieldwork experience represented in the vast amounts of data gathered into journal articles. Questions such as the following emerge: What do I want to write about? On which aspects of the data do I focus? How do I construct a compelling argument? How do I reduce what I have to say so that it fits into a journal-sized article? What did I find most interesting and how does it link with theory? How do I depict the actual complexity of life that occurred in the organization? For us, the difficult questions have centered on: How do we see the most interesting questions arising from our research? How do we choose the best theoretical location for our work? How do we convey the meaning of our work—its significance and import—so that it resonates with readers? Ten years later, we continue to grapple with these questions, but we now appreciate that it is just the "nature of the beast" when we adopt a qualitative unstructured approach to inquiry.

Since the first edition of the book, understanding of the interpretive turn toward language has matured (Bruner, 1996; Clifford & Marcus, 1986; Geertz, 1983, 1988; Rabinow & Sullivan, 1987; Rorty, 1989), as has awareness and concern with the writing project and how we narrate our research. Whereas little discussion and few, if any, courses existed in doctoral programs then, today, there is some consideration of writing as part of the professional development of faculty (Boice, 2000). Furthermore, in those institutions in which qualitative research has a strong tradition, courses concerned with representation are available. However, as a foundational activity of our profession, writing continues to be insufficiently discussed. This paucity of attention to writing occurs at the cost of individual and collective wisdom. In neglecting matters of writing, we impoverish our capacity to generate theoretically relevant insights from everyday life.

We write this edition of the book for several reasons. First, we write to consolidate and reflect our refined understanding of the task of writing qualitative research articles, building on the increasing appreciation of the artful side (Gubrium & Holstein, 1997) of producing disciplinary texts. Second, we write to provide an update on the state of qualitative writing and, in particular, to recognize and reflect on examples of the variety of qualitative research that has proliferated in our journals. Third, during the past decade, the popularity of qualitative research has continued to grow and to spread across disciplines. It has been adopted in communities in which, in the early 1990s, few qualitative studies appeared, such as Information Systems. Recognizing this, we write to explicitly expand our consideration of qualitative writing in journals to incorporate work from two additional disciplines in which it has burgeoned—Information Systems and Health Studies.

We continue to imagine you, the reader, as similar to those people with whom we have had and continue to have conversations about writing our research for publication. You are likely to be graduate students who are learning about qualitative research and writing issues for the first time, as well as more seasoned qualitative researchers who are exploring ways to become more reflective about what you are doing. We expect that those of you who will find this book most interesting and useful will be right in the throes of writing up fieldwork or proposals for research projects, or those of you reflecting more generally on the writing process.

WRITING ABOUT WRITING

When we wrote the first edition, we noted several authors who had already written about writing and who had informed our perspectives. Some of these authors offered practical guidance for the writing process. A book by the sociologist Howard Becker (1986) concretely examined the mechanics of the writing process, including the underlying fears about writing and social organization conventions that hinder clarity in writing. Another sociologist, Gary Alan Fine (1988), developed ten practical "commandments" about writing. In particular, he emphasized that, because all writing is socially situated, social scientists should have particular audiences and purposes in mind as they write. He also encouraged researchers to use literary techniques such as metaphors and poetic language to bring an argument to life for readers. Wolcott (1990, 2001) developed some hands-on and very useful suggestions for moving along the writing process in its various phases, as reflected by his chapter titles: getting going, keeping going, tightening up, finishing up and getting published. Continuing in this tradition, Huff (1998) outlines a step-by-step approach to the writing process that begins with choosing a subject and ends with a manuscript submitted for publication. She emphasizes the importance of writing in a way that is consistent with the rules of having good conversations.

Participating in the interpretive turn (Bruner, 1996; Geertz, 1983, 1988; Rabinow & Sullivan, 1987) with its attendant concern with language and the construction of meaning, other authors had turned their attention to the texts researchers produced and examined their narrative strategies and textual practices. Gephart (1986, 1988) examined rhetorical conventions, for example the use of passive or quasi-passive voice and the creation of gaps, to support and legitimate arguments based on quantitative data. The work by Van Maanen (1988, 1995) and Geertz (1988) examined the narrative strategies associated with ethnographic writing. Since that time, other authors have made important contributions. Ellis and Bochner (1996) produced and collected a range of writing that experimented with various textual forms in order to deliberately push the boundary on conventions for disciplinary texts. Focusing on narrative as one facet of the interpretive turn in social sciences, Czarniawska (1999, 2004) examined the use and analysis of narrative in scientific practice, including writing endeavors.

In writing this revision, we continue in the intellectual tradition represented by these works. How critical it is to have an emerging tradition of writing about writing to draw upon! As well, the intellectual foundation for this edition of the book continues to be informed by rhetoric and literary theory in the social sciences. In particular, we have been influenced by the work of Booth (1961, 1967) and Iser (1978, 1989), who have incorporated into literary criticism the notions of implied author and reader and active texts and readers; by the work of Knorr-Cetina (1981), Latour (1987), and Latour and Woolgar (1986), who have examined scientific texts as part of their investigations of science in action; and by the work of Bazerman and his colleagues (Bazerman, 1988; Bazerman & Paradis, 1991; Bazerman & Prior, 2004), McCloskey

(1985, 1990, 1994), Selzer (1993), and Winsor (1996), who have examined directly the rhetorical dimension and textual practices of disciplinary texts.

Our book also differs from the above work in that we seek to provide a systematic, yet very concrete approach to composing qualitative research. Although we definitely bring a literary and rhetorical understanding to this book, we seek to integrate this knowledge and perspective into specific and critical issues that we, as writers, face in constructing written accounts of our fieldwork. In doing so, our major focus concerns how to convert our field engagement into theoretically relevant insights and claims to an audience based in our relevant professional community.

WRITING OUR FIELDWORK

After some seventeen or so years of thinking, reading, researching and writing about writing, we now take for granted that efforts to transform qualitative research efforts into written textual form concern much more than the rational presentation of data. Composing qualitative research is not a linear process in which we gather "facts" in the field that speak for themselves and make our contribution apparent to all readers (see Becker, 1986, and Feldman, 1995, for discussions of this).

From the perspective we occupy today, we believe that the major tasks of writing with qualitative data involve connecting the field and academic worlds via literature-based ideas that illuminate insights garnered in the field and produce knowledge claims viewed as unique contributions by the relevant professional community of readers. We do not simply present facts that stand alone, but rather craft arguments intended to persuade readers that we have something new to offer relative to extant literature. At the personal level, the crafting and shaping of the manuscript involves ourselves as authors; the research setting, including members with whom we interacted for longer or shorter periods of time; the arguments we make and how we develop them in the text; and our informal as well as formal interactions with colleagues and members of our communities around our developing stories. At a more general, though nevertheless influential level, our writing task takes into consideration the academic institutional setting, with its associated norms for "doing science" and journal review processes, and our largely academic community of readers.

FOCUS ON "THEORIZED STORYLINE"

So, how do we craft a manuscript that brings together the academic and field worlds to develop theoretically relevant insights regarded as a contribution? In the first edition of this book, we called upon the metaphor of "story" to illuminate matters of writing for management journals. By invoking this metaphor, we were better able to draw attention to *how* we write, and to begin to explicate what it takes to compose qualitative research for our journals.

In this second edition, we have retained and elaborated the narrative perspective. The distinguishing characteristic of stories is that they possess a discernible framework for structuring the written account. Stories are grounded in events, and provide a narrative structure that organizes those events into some arrangement of the past, present and future. Further, they provide an explanation of the turn of events through the development of a plot. Whereas in the first edition we developed the idea of story, but only implicitly incorporated storyline, in this edition we explicitly develop storyline as a narrative device that helps us write together the field and academic worlds.

One day, while we were writing the first edition of this book, Karen Locke's young (at that time!) son, Ian, showed her a picture that he had drawn in school that day. The picture portrayed a snowman and had three separate scenes representing the narrative structure of the story that Ian had crafted. The first scene showed a snowman with a top hat and smile. The second scene introduced the sun, along with the snowman as he had looked in the first scene. In the final scene, the sun was still shining, but all that remained of the snowman was a puddle and the top hat.

This story still is relevant, but now our interpretation focuses more on storyline. Very simply, yet elegantly, Ian's story of the snowman showed not only the chronological progression of events over time, but also potential storylines that explained the turn of events involving the snowman and the sun: the introduction of the sun had caused the snowman to melt; the appearance of the sun threatened the very life of the snowman; life can present precarious situations, and so on.

Similarly, as qualitative researchers, we observe organizational events and members' interpretations of those events as they unfold. Indeed, what we offer in the way of distinctive knowledge is a view of events in organizations as process- and meaning based; we are uniquely situated to contribute to knowledge about how organizational phenomena occur, as well as what those phenomena mean. As qualitative researchers, we convert our engagement with this field into theoretical insights and ideas of interest and import to a disciplinary audience. We accomplish this by articulating a *theorized storyline,* or a particular kind of plot that relates the field and academic worlds. Thus, we link organizational members' actions and interpretations of what happened with theoretical discussions to generate possible claims concerning what might have happened. In the case of the snowman, for example, we might momentarily imagine the snowman as organization and link the field complication of the sun melting the snowman to some theoretical discourse. So, we could offer knowledge claims about how organizations are strategically vulnerable to certain aspects of the environment, or that a liability of newness exists for young organizations in turbulent environments.

By invoking the metaphor of stories and drawing attention to the importance of generating theorized storylines, we more readily notice "how" we write, and are better able to integrate it with the "what" of our writing. For example, we notice: (1) how extant literature looks *before* the proposed study, including significantly its gaps or omissions; (2) how extant literature looks *after* the proposed study, including changes that result from addressing the gaps; and (3) how the insights garnered *along the way* shed theoretical light and significance on the complications faced by actors in the field. Similarly, Weick (1995) suggests that, "In a full defense of an idea, the author shows how some display looks different before and after it is viewed using the innovation that is proposed."

Finally, by invoking story and theorized storyline, we also draw attention to the significant social dimension of composing our manuscripts in disciplinary communities. For example, we begin to discern the complexities and nuances associated with how we craft our character as scientific storytellers. How do we establish our character in the texts we write, and how does what we produce persuade our disciplinary readers to regard or disregard our claims? We also notice the important task of *re*-writing that accompanies our manuscripts' journeys from initial sharing of ideas to eventual publication of those ideas in our disciplinary journals. Along the way, our ideas and theorized storylines can undergo significant shaping!

ORGANIZATION OF CHAPTERS

We have maintained the metaphor of story in the organization of this edition of the book. Chapter 1, "The Style and Practice of Our Academic Writing," explores taken-for-granted assumptions in our profession that influence, and more particularly, mystify the process of writing up qualitative research. It also provides a framework for thinking about composing qualitative research for journal publication. Specifically, it suggests our major writing task is to convert our engagement with the field into theoretical insights and ideas of interest and import to a disciplinary audience. In Chapter 2, "Crafting a Theorized Storyline," we draw on the metaphor of plot to introduce the idea that we accomplish this writing task by articulating a *theorized storyline*, or a particular kind of plot that relates the field and academic worlds. It highlights four rhetorical moves authors use in establishing theorized storylines in their manuscripts: articulating study significance, situating the study in the literature, problematizing the literature through gap creation, and making space for the study to contribute by foreshadowing how it addresses the problematization. Chapter 3, "Developing the Theorized Storyline," examines how authors draw on the rich, specific descriptions of everyday life in organizations to illuminate the theoretical significance of complications faced by actors in the field. We show how, in developing their theorized storylines for journal articles comprised of limited space, authors have produced some innovation in representing field data. Chapter 4, "Characterizing the Storyteller," shows how authors construct the storyteller in journal articles. Reflecting the impact of the interpretive turn on authors' portrayals of themselves in published studies, it highlights the question of who we want to be in our writing. It examines how, in addition to depicting the character of the institutional scientists in their texts, authors are increasingly revealing their human face. Chapter 5, "Re-Writing the Story," has been reframed to more explicitly consider our writing efforts as a social process, focusing on how members of our academic community participate in our writing as we craft and re-craft our manuscripts on their journey to publication. This edition extends in three respects our profile of manuscripts along the way to publication. First, we have incorporated the journeys of seven additional articles (for a total of 13) via interviews with the authors and materials of the review process for these articles, including reviewer and editor comments. Second, through these interviews, we provide a glimpse into the critical arena of sharing early drafts of manuscripts prior to submitting them for formal review. Finally, the comments from editors and reviewers, as well as author responses, enable us to extend the portrait of exchanges during the formal review process that shape and negotiate the writing of the manuscript. Finally, in "Concluding Comments," we share some closing thoughts on writing matters.

In each chapter, we use actual examples from published writings drawn from mainstream journals in Management, Information Systems, and Health Studies. As well, in keeping with the informal style of writing we use in this book, we reference the authors of these works by using both their last and their (usually more informal) first names. Each of these examples uses wholly qualitative data in its presentation. No particular criteria were applied to the selection of the articles discussed, except that they illustrated especially well the aspect of writing under discussion. The examples are by no means exhaustive. As you read, we would hope that both your knowledge and repertoire of others' qualitative work, as well as your own work, will provide additional illustrations.

The final caution we issued in our first edition still holds: Throughout our writing of this book, we have been well aware of two primary and sometimes conflicting motivations. On the one hand, we want to provide especially first-time researchers with support to make the transition from the field to writing a creative, rather than debilitating one. To this end, throughout the book we identify and illustrate a number of rhetorical practices that authors use to craft and develop their theoretical insights. On the other hand, we want to avoid espousing a normative "how-to" guide or boilerplate approach to composing qualitative research. We are not advocating one right or correct way to write up data. To do so would dampen the creativity in each person's writing adventures, resulting in increasingly uninteresting and similar work. So, in this book we have sought very intentionally to examine what a wide variety of authors using qualitative data in journals are up to in their work. The outcome, we hope, is that as conscious writers and readers of the theorized storylines we craft, we will all contribute to the generation of knowledge that is more imaginative, thoughtful, reasoned and insightful.

ONE

THE STYLE AND PRACTICE
OF OUR ACADEMIC WRITING

———•◦•———

W riting this book underscores that whatever else we may be as researchers and scholars, we are at the core a profession of text writers. The knowledge our various disciplines have assembled about organizations is composed and maintained in written texts. As scholars who study organizational phenomena, our research efforts are known, in large part, through our written products. The papers and monographs we write stand symbolically for the data gathering and analytic efforts we put into our scholarship. In addition, as we are all too aware, our ability to be individual members in good standing in the profession revolves around the ability to write our disciplines' texts; our careers, visibility, and professional mobility are all implicated in our writing (Frost & Taylor, 1995).

Indeed, knowledge-creating professions (Bazerman & Paradis, 1991) constitute themselves and maintain organization and power through networks of texts, such as journals, books, newsletters, that frame and select the topics and issues paid attention to. In addition, those individuals who are in positions to decide on the disposition of these texts, such as editors and members of editorial boards, are widely viewed as enjoying considerable professional power. Moreover, embedded in these texts are taken-for-granted assumptions, a field's normative traditions, concerning what we write and how we do so. Like it or not—and sometimes we do and sometimes we don't—in this profession, we are about writing. And this writing sets the terms of much of our work lives.

Yet, in spite of the pervasiveness and significance of writing in our professional lives, there remains a troubling absence of discussion about writing. Very few books and articles, and even fewer formal disciplinary forums examine the writing endeavor. Significantly, this ignorance about writing occurs at our disciplinary peril. When we overlook and compartmentalize the writing enterprise, we constrain our abilities to portray situated human life in work organizations and to develop new lines of sight in our theorizing efforts (Locke, Golden-Biddle, & Feldman, 2004).

Consequently, in this first chapter, we look directly at the "writing" enterprise in the context of our professional activities. Our discussion juxtaposes the predominant style of writing that we find in journal articles as unadorned and disembodied, with the experienced nature of writing as a complex practice in the process of creating knowledge. In doing so, we hope to provoke and open up dialogue on what we take for granted in our writing activity.

THE PREDOMINANT STYLE OF ACADEMIC WRITING: UNADORNED AND DISEMBODIED

What is this genre known as a research article, which is the major form of communicating knowledge in many scientific disciplines? What kind of writing distinguishes it? The more typical answer is that academic writing in journals is a straightforward account of researchers' investigations of some aspect of organizational life. Socialized into our disciplinary community, we come to understand this writing as an impersonal and detached demonstration of the results of our investigative procedures, as well as an explanation of the work's significance to existing knowledge.

Following conventions in the "sciences," the writing in these reports is generally taken to be minimally expressive so that discovered phenomena can be reflected as clearly as possible in the text. This is a "windowpane" model of language (Brooks & Warren, 1938) in which scientists carefully avoid in their scientific prose "all associations, emotional coloring, and implications of attitude and judgment" (Brooks & Warren, 1938, p. 4). Such non-ornamental prose is well suited to an understanding of the journal article's function as transferring information gleaned from the field to the library—that academically removed knowledge repository. This Kantian perspective on writing, as Richard Rorty points out, construes writing as an "unfortunate necessity" (1982, p. 94), a sort of reluctant intermediary between an investigated field and disciplinary knowledge. Similar views have been articulated by scholars who study organizational phenomena. For example, Pinder and Bourgeois (1982, p. 646) urge researchers to "deliberately strive" to avoid all literary tropes in their writing in order to "tie scientific communication to observable phenomena by way of direct reference and ostentation." These authors urge us to tell the simple truth, plain and unvarnished, about the aspects of organizational life we observe.

EXPERIENCING THE PRACTICE OF ACADEMIC WRITING

Yet, experiences indicate that the practice of academic writing is neither plain nor simple. It is a way of writing that we have had to learn. Based on discussions with colleagues over the years, we suspect that very few of us start out by knowing how to write the "academic speak" of our profession. Rather, we become socialized into the language and writing practices that symbolize the culture of science and that are traditionally transmitted across generations of academics.

For example, as members of the profession, we pick up that special anonymous disciplinary code in which "it is concluded that," and only "the data," not researchers, "suggest" anything. Yet, extensive use of the passive voice keeps the researcher out of the text (Gephart, 1986) as well as makes the writing cumbersome and obtuse. During graduate studies, Karen Locke can remember submitting a course paper in which she was present in the first person, "I, therefore, conclude . . . ," only to be told that it was unacceptable. Being present in the text in that way was a violation of the professional code that required her to write in the disembodied voice of scientific demonstration. She had to learn to write herself out of her texts and let "the findings speak for themselves." By doing so, she symbolically adhered to, and transmitted, the view of writing as straightforward reporting of observed phenomena.

Certainly, if the writing of scientific work does not come naturally, then neither does the reading of it for audiences outside these disciplinary boundaries. As we are all too well aware, many of the practices associated with the scientific style obfuscate our points. Ironically, the straightforward reporting that is a hallmark of academic writing is anything but straightforward! This inaccessibility of our writing is particularly troublesome in applied disciplines like management, health, or information technology where we often have two audiences for our work. Presumably, we would like not only academics, but also professionals and managers to read and comment on our work. Paradoxically, in conforming to our implicit assumptions regarding a scientific style of writing, our writing may well discourage other audiences from engaging it.

In the years since we first began to write about writing, doctoral students in particular have shared with us their experiences in learning how to write in the academic style. Recently, in conducting a doctoral class on writing, we asked students to share their experiences of writing in the academy. Here is some of what they had to say as they worked to satisfy the demands of producing this particular writing genre.

> The [academic] paper is a much more lengthy writing process than my earlier writing. . . . So, many times I find it to be a daunting task to sit down and write.

> Writing the scholarly paper is definitely challenging for me because it is quite alien to the way I generally write. I didn't know where and how to incorporate my insight and the template was something that made me write in a very conscious manner; hence I was never happy with the way the paper flowed.

> It is somewhat mechanical in nature, and in many ways restricting.

> Sometimes I felt that what I really wanted to say or communicate never came through in the final draft. The language is still a bit alien to me, so it's not by nature that I think in those words. When I write what I want to express the way that I am most comfortable, it seems really simplistic and not scholarly enough.

> I struggle with how well the ideas should be developed before starting to write. I lose ideas that aren't written down clearly.

> This work is different from what I did earlier because then I didn't think I had to confine myself to any particular theoretical framework. . . . There was no particular template that my paper had to conform to, nor any definite style to adopt.

As readily discerned in our discussion thus far, disciplinary writing is neither plain nor simple and straightforward. Rather, like the work of writing more generally (Dillard, 1989; Elbow, 1981; Lamott, 1995), it is highly particular, demanding, and complex professional work. As noted by others, it is also a more social, complicated, and human performance than the prevailing narrow positivist conception allows (Czarniawska, 1999; Hunter, 1990; Richardson, 1990). When we sit in front of our terminals with our piles of field notes, transcripts, and analytic memos, expecting to "just write it up," as Van Maanen (1988) indicates he was told to do, we discover all too clearly that it's not that simple. Writing is far from an easy, "isn't-it-obvious" process, and in implying such, the injunction to "just write it up" masks the choices, challenges, joys, and frustrations involved in composing qualitative research.

Write It Up, But *What* Do We Write?

First, this injunction implies that the meaning around which the manuscript will be oriented lies already formed, waiting to be picked up. Yet, what we convey in our writing is not the stream of recorded conversations and actions, nor the carefully produced analytic tables, but rather the significance of these details of organization life for broader phenomena, processes, and theories. Contrary to the windowpane assumptions of findings as self-evident, we never yet have had a piece of data tell us its significance!

As well, the injunction belies the artful and often arduous process of writing the field data for what they all mean. As we work with the field notes, transcripts, and analytic memoranda through which we document and pattern our experience in the field, what we are doing is thinking about that experience in order to make some sense out of it and to gain some insight into particular phenomena, processes, and theories. In our sensemaking efforts, we think about the field experience in relation to other comparable situations, and in relation to what other researchers and scholars have said about similar situations. Conversely, we also think about other researchers' theories in light of our particular experiences. We do not write up all that we saw, heard, or were told. Rather, we write up what all of our thinking and comparing has led us to believe our field experience means (Watson, 1995) for our understanding.

Furthermore, even after we discern meaning in and derive insights from our fieldwork, we still encounter difficulties. This is especially the case when we write journal articles. Typically, our data surface many issues that we find important and worthy of telling. However, because a journal article imposes significant spatial constraints on our writing, we cannot tell all the meanings and insights we discerned; we must make choices. In a real sense, we have to set aside aspects of our investigative experience that, although important to us and even integral to our experiences of field life, do not help us to develop the particular meanings and insights we have chosen to write about. The tradeoff between conveying some or all of the meaning discerned in the field experience stands in starkest relief when we write for journals with space limitations; though it is also present to a lesser degree in writing books.

For Karen Golden-Biddle, this tradeoff is most vivid. Although she has published from her dissertation fieldwork (Golden, 1992), she has had difficulty figuring out how to tell in journal article form what, to her, is the central insight from her fieldwork; that in a large, Fortune 500 organization, managers appreciate the practices and beliefs developed by past generations of managers, and actively transmit and seek to enact them in the present. Early manuscripts telling this story met with colleague skepticism. How, they question, can a Fortune 500 organization survive in today's changing environment when it is oriented to the past? For her, an important difficulty in telling this story is the lack of space in a journal article to sufficiently detail what constitutes the traditional cornerstone of this organization while articulating the most insightful theoretical storyline.

To the extent that we choose to develop and write about particular meanings disclosed in our fieldwork, we obviously regard what we write about as constructed. Few among us today would accept the proposition that researchers go into the field to gather up the pieces of reality lying around waiting to be gleaned. We appreciate instead that researchers, as well as organization members, shape the experienced reality. In much the same way, we reject the notion of writing as a transmission of an objective reality. We agree with the literary critics Booth (1961) and Iser (1978, 1989); sociologists Bochner and Ellis (1996), Gusfield (1981), and Richardson (1990, 1994); and management theorists Czarniawska (1999, 2004) and Van Maanen (1995) that the hand of the writer and the eyes of the reader shape all written work, even that in science. Our written products are crafted works.

Write It Up, But *For Whom* Do We Write?

The injunction also conceals the readers for whom we write: the particular disciplinary community making up the audience for the journal article. As such, our audience is a sort of a concealed, though highly significant participant in the writing process. There's no getting around it; all manuscripts are addressed to a particular audience (Burke, 1950; Booth, 1961; Iser, 1978;

Richardson, 1990). When we choose to direct our work toward mainstream academic journals, we privilege an academic audience over others. In turn, our selected audience exerts its influence over our writing. Our professional community sets the topical boundaries for our writing, broadly delimiting the phenomena that fall within a selected domain of study. Our audience also broadly sets out manuscript structure and progression: the movement from literature review, to methods, results, and a concluding discussion. Those disciplinary writing conventions allow readers to consider our work as coming from one who is a member of the scientific community. To shun the use of such established forms and formats is potentially to deny our work a forum within the profession (Lyne, 1993).

So, we address the research findings to a general audience of scholars studying organizational phenomena who, as we have indicated, have their own compositional conventions and, of course, insider language. But more specifically, with regard to any given manuscript, we write for an audience of researchers and scholars also interested in the particular organizational processes, phenomena, and theories addressed by the putative work. Our respective discipline, like any other disciplinary community, is composed of small overlapping social systems delineated by interest in a particular phenomenon or idea, "'specialties,' 'problem domains,' 'research areas,' 'research networks'" (Knorr-Cetina, 1981, p. 9) or "schools of thought" (McKinley, Mone, & Moon, 1999; Ofori-Dankwa & Julian, 2005). Typically, our work is directed toward one or perhaps two of these specialty audiences.

Again, some examples might clarify. Karen Locke can still quite vividly remember sitting with pages and pages of carefully worked out analyses, documenting and explaining the patterning of comedic episodes in a tertiary care hospital (Locke, 1996). Certainly, she had a tale to tell about doctors, patient anxiety, and comedy; the topic of organizational humor had received only scattered and erratic attention. She had a tale for which only a small, some would say marginal, audience existed—as the very modest literature on organizational humor attests. However, she demarcated a broader audience for the work by recasting doctors as service providers and patients as coproviders in the service delivery process, and by embedding a research account about one aspect of hospital life in a broader discussion of emotionality in client-provider relationships.

Karen Golden-Biddle remembers conversations with Trish Reay and Kathy GermAnn that focused on how best to tell the story of a change initiative in a health organization that was undertaken by active and persistent individuals across organizational levels. They had pages of data and analyses of individuals' efforts and actions. Highlighting the agency of these individuals as internal actors who were implementing macro-level change enabled them to demarcate an audience for the work in organizational and institutional change (Reay, Golden-Biddle, & GermAnn, 2006).

Thus, writing necessarily incorporates the question, For whom do we write? The meanings we choose to develop and articulate in our work must be directed toward and lay claim to a specific audience within the disciplinary community. Furthermore, while an audience finds engaging the details of work life in particular organizations that qualitative research yields—whether those details describe an Israeli high-tech corporation (Ailon-Souday & Kunda, 2003); a funeral home (Barley, 1983); a publicly funded teaching hospital in Australia (Cheek & Gibson, 2003); a corporation's Web site (Coupland & Brown, 2004); large, international manufacturing companies (Markus, Majchrzak, & Gasser, 2002); community-based family practice organizations (Miller, Crabtree, McDaniel, & Stange, 1998); the emergency departments of level 1 trauma centers (Morse & Pooler, 2002); a large software company headquartered in The Netherlands (Orlikowski, 2002); a bill collection agency (Sutton, 1991); and so on—our disciplinary audiences are primarily motivated by interest in theory. Such audiences, constituted along particular theoretical lines, are interested in these details, but primarily as they relate to theory (Langer, 1964). Our disciplinary manuscripts are addressed toward particular theoretical lines that interest us and our readers.

Becker (1986), Huff (1998), McCloskey (1990), Rankin (2001), and others use the metaphor of a conversation to describe the theoretical interests and literature-building activities of our disciplinary audience. As members of academic communities, we have audiences interested in and writing about a broad range of topics and issues, including high-technology acquisitions and knowledge transfer (Ranft & Lord, 2002), the introduction of change in primary care practices (Miller et al., 1998), the relationship between technology and structure (Barley, 1986), suffering and the construction of self (Charmaz, 1999), the decision-making process involved in the search and selection of aged care facilities (Cheek & Ballantyne, 2001), and so on. When we write our work, we use the discussion of existing literature to locate the study in a particular conversation. Yet we are not just looking to join or eavesdrop on (Becker, 1986) these conversations. Rather, we need to create space to make our own contributions (Locke & Golden-Biddle, 1997; Mone & McKinley, 1993). As researchers working with qualitative data, we bring together the meanings and insights from our experiences in the field with the various possible theoretical conversations to help produce and shape the literatures of interest.

Write It Up, But *Under What Terms* Will Our Writing Be Granted a Disciplinary Audience?

Finally, the injunction to write it up veils the terms under which our work will be given a reading by a particular community of scholars. We do not join and contribute to the literature until our work is published, and disciplinary communities have admission requirements for inclusion in this "public" theoretical discourse. Certainly the work must be judged to be in some sense "true," that is, to authentically depict the situation studied (Golden-Biddle & Locke, 1993), but it must also be significant. As researchers, we must craft our experience in the field so as to contribute theoretically; to make a difference in extant literature (Golden-Biddle & Locke, 1993; Locke & Golden-Biddle, 1997).

Taken all together, then, the injunction to write it up conceals how we shape field notes and analytic memoranda in light of existing work in our academic discipline. It also masks the considerable work involved in the crafting of our story; how we integrate and develop theory and insights derived from our engagement with the field to make a difference in, and contribute to disciplinary writing. Ultimately, the injunction masks the production of research reports as human constructions intended to persuade a particular community that what they have to say is both "true" and important to the domains we study. In unmasking and unpacking "just write it up," then, we see that individual researchers shape and form the findings, invoke and delimit an audience who will be interested in the work, and seek to convince the audience that their work makes a difference in our understanding of a particular organizational phenomenon. Writing is thus revealed to be a much more active, creative, and human process than the "window pane" model would have us believe.

THE STYLE AND PRACTICE OF ACADEMIC WRITING: INTERESTED AND PERSUASIVE DISCOURSE

As our preceding discussion hints, even when our research articles provide coherent stories that point to particular theoretical contributions, they are not automatically construed as knowledge. They have to be accorded the status of knowledge, that is, be seen as true and significant, first by a small group of reviewers representing our disciplinary community, and then by the wider community itself. What counts as knowledge, then, is a matter of disciplinary consensus (Aronson, 1984; Latour, 1987; Latour & Woolgar, 1986; Rorty, 1967). Whether the research will count as knowledge or not depends on whether it is subsequently incorporated into other research reports as part of the literature review summarizing what we know about a given topic. Only when it is cited, and its findings are used in future published papers, will a piece of research have achieved the status of contributing to knowledge in the field. If intended readers seriously challenge it, or even worse, completely ignore it, then its claim of knowledge will have been denied (Gilbert, 1976; Winsor, 1993).

Accordingly, we can view journal articles as proposals directed to particular audiences for them to legitimate our grounded and theoretically relevant claims as knowledge (Aronson, 1984; Gilbert, 1976). As proposals of knowledge, they require adjudication and some accrediting action on the part of their disciplinary audience before they are accorded the status of knowledge. When we submit and publish our work, then, we are putting out proposals that constitute a link between us as authors and our audience (Cozzens, 1985). Further, our knowledge proposals are constructed as, and intended to be taken as, authoritative (Spector & Kitsuse, 1977). Our authority to write is disclosed in the presentation of "data-informed insights," in the author's exposition of the history of knowledge development in the area (as well as delineation of problems in it), in the account of the investigative and analytic operations performed, and so on.

In addition, we do not simply lay out knowledge proposals for our audience to take or leave. As we have already indicated, our audience's accrediting actions are highly sought after. We write from an interested perspective; we have a personal stake in the outcomes of our work. At the same time that we write to explicate our theoretically relevant insights, we write to shape and advance them as claims to knowledge. We construct our research products with an eye toward audience reaction, and in so doing, write to persuade others of the contribution of our work.

Interestingly, until the late 1970s, most academicians considered scientific texts to be nonpersuasive. Science was viewed as a special discourse operating outside the domain of rhetoric (Selzer, 1993). Whereas artists were thought to persuade through language, scientists were thought to persuade through logic and evidence (Gusfield, 1981). Rhetoric was and, unfortunately still today, is considered something of a dirty word: one that automatically invokes the qualifying adjectives *mere* and *empty*. This image of rhetoric, however, rests on an essentially monologic view of texts (Billig, 1993; Mulkay, 1995). It presents authors as omnipotent, delivering their powerful words to a hapless readership who can only deliver up their highly sought accreditation with "tears, cheers, and helpless admiration" (Billig, 1993, p. 122). What a glorious writer's fantasy! Of course, this distorted image of rhetoric overestimates the effect our texts have on our readers at the same time that it underestimates the effect our readers have on our texts.

For some time now, the view of scientific writing as a-rhetorical has been challenged by an understanding of such writing as indeed rhetorical by virtue of its constructing theoretical arguments intended for an audience (McCloskey, 1994). During the past decades, a number of disciplines have turned a rhetorical lens on their own writing practices. For example, research traditions and new conversations have developed in anthropology (Clifford, 1983; Geertz, 1973, 1988; Marcus, 1980; Marcus & Cushman, 1982; Marcus & Fischer, 1986), in economics (McCloskey, 1985, 1994), and in sociology (Atkinson, 1990; Edmonson, 1984; Hunter, 1990). More recently, organizational scholars, too, have analyzed their own texts (Calas & Smircich, 1991; Czarniawska, 1999, 2004; Golden-Biddle & Locke, 1993; Kilduff, 1993; Locke & Golden-Biddle, 1997; Mumby & Putnam, 1992; Van Maanen, 1988, 1995; Watson, 1995).

The above authors have noted that, even when we adhere in our writing to the strictest conventions of science, even when we remove all personal associations, use technical terms, rely very heavily on presented data, and so on, our texts are nevertheless persuasive. They persuade our audience that we are competent scientists whose work and findings are credible. For example, when Knorr-Cetina (1981) describes how research chemists fashion a textual linearity out of a nonlinear research process, she provides an example of how these authors persuade by adhering to the conventions of presenting the research process. Similarly, March and Simon's (1958) foundational text, *Organizations*, has been praised for its avoidance of rhetorical devices like figurative language (Pinder & Bourgeois, 1982). However, as Kilduff's (1993) analysis of this work aptly demonstrates, while the authors clearly stated that they were sacrificing the literary in favor of a scientific style, they nonetheless relied on various textual strategies to configure as severely limited and inadequate, prior research and theorizing on organizations. There is no escaping rhetoric in our writing. As soon as we frame ideas and craft theoretically relevant insights into claims for presentation to some audience, we are engaging in rhetoric or persuasive discourse.

Paying attention to the textual construction of our grounded theoretical insights does not undermine their truth value. Such attention simply provides us a more sophisticated perspective from which to read, and to write, them. Our choice does not concern whether to write persuasive discourse. That is given. Instead, it concerns how conscious we will become of our rhetorical efforts in knowledge making. Incorporating a rhetorical understanding in our work enables us to demystify and become more reflexive about our own and others' writing. It also better situates us to look outward and make a difference in our writing. We agree in this regard with Bazerman (1996), who adeptly articulates,

> We have so stigmatized rhetoric and so compartmentalized our ideas of writing that we only engage in the great welter of our communicative world behind our intellectual backs. Our ideals of knowledge that escape the particularity of our human circumstances are so strong that those who call our attention to the creative role of situated strategic communication seem to do so only to debunk those institutions that produce knowledge and authority. But to examine carefully and sympathetically the rhetorical travels of knowledge in society is not to debunk our ideals of knowledge, but to understand more about the possibility of knowledge to make a difference in the world . . . (p. viii)

Indeed, for those who read disciplinary texts with an eye on their textual practices, it does not take long to discern literary elements. These range from those that are quite small to others that are more figural in the text. Let's consider some examples that provide a taste of the relationship between the disciplinary knowledge we generate and how we use language to convey that knowledge. As an illustration of more diminutive literary elements, look at the use of a single qualifying word to help the following articles construct consensual theoretical positions within various conversations (Locke & Golden-Biddle, 1997).

> Many researchers have commented on the poor fit between the requirements of processes with the characteristics of EKPs [emergent knowledge processes] . . . and existing IT application types, such as executive information systems (EIS) and expert systems (ES). For example . . . (from Markus, Majchrzak, & Gasser, 2002, p. 184)

> There is a considerable literature on the importance of workplace relationships for individuals' careers . . . (from Gersick, Bartunek, & Dutton, 2000, pp. 1026–1027)

The resistance of clinical practices and physicians' behavior to change is well documented . . . (from Miller et al., 1998, p. 370)

There is considerable agreement among those who have studied mentoring that in order to understand fully the nature and impact of this developmental relationship, it is necessary to examine how it changes over time . . . (from Kram, 1983, p. 609)

A growing amount of literature suggests that organizational identifications are important for both individuals' and organizations' well-being . . . (from Elsbach & Bhattacharya, 2001, p. 393)

Theorists largely agree that individual power in organizations is the ability to control others, to exercise discretion, to get one's own way. (from Biggart & Hamilton, 1984, p. 540)

In the above examples, the authors assert that scholars share similar perspectives about some aspect of organizational life in order to theoretically position their own study. Accordingly, the use of the qualifiers, *considerable . . . largely . . . many . . . virtually . . . well . . . growing,* in each of these claims permits the authors to highlight that significant agreement does indeed exist among scholars, without, of course, asserting that the stated claims are unassailable.

A more familiar literary device is the use of metaphor, depicted below in three examples. The first example, from an article by Connie Gersick (1988), challenges extant group development models based on a hierarchical progression of groups through universal stages, and proposes as replacement, the "punctuated" model. To highlight the distinction between the two models, she draws on the metaphor of a football game to underscore what she found:

It was like seeing the game of football as progressing through a structure of quarters (phases) with a major half-time break, versus seeing the game as progressing in a characteristic sequence of distinguishable styles of play (stages). (p. 16)

This literary device is used both to portray the essential properties of her proposed model and to distinguish it from the prevailing model. At the same time that the metaphor helps to convey the results and theoretical implications of her research inquiries (a phase vs. stage perspective), it also proposes them as a new contribution to the literature on group development.

A second example occurs in the article by Sue Llewellyn (2001), who uses the metaphor, two-way window, as an analytic device to understand the increasingly mediated space between medical and management work. She explains her use of this metaphor as follows,

> In this paper, sets of ideas are either embodied in a person—the clinical director—or embedded in an object—the budget. Clinical directors as "two-way windows" are mediating persons as they work through sets of ideas belonging to management and sets of ideas belonging to clinical practice; they will only have a coherent perspective, if these sets of ideas undergo some mutual adaptation. In the process of the budget becoming a "two-way window," ideas from the world of management and ideas from the world of the clinician become more consistent, in order for the budget to become a coherent object with which both managers and clinicians can work. (p. 602)

In using this metaphor, she highlights and theorizes the role of clinicians (here, physicians) who assume management responsibilities such as budgeting, and more generally the various possibilities for action when the boundaries become more permeable between managers and professionals.

A final example concerns the characterization of the stigma felt by leaders of bankrupt firms:

> Tom was extremely nervous. He cleared his throat over and over again. He chain-smoked. He was hunched over. His hands and voice trembled. And, he made an odd sort of hissing noise over and over. He looked psychologically beaten. I felt like a voyeur, spying on Willy Loman. (from Sutton & Callahan, 1987, p. 421)

The authors advance a theory about how bankruptcy spoils the image of organizations and of their top managers. The graphic and dramatic portrayal of organization leaders, as intensely affected by their company's Chapter 11 status, helps to underscore the importance of studying the stigma associated with bankruptcy. This could hardly be better accomplished than by comparing "Tom" to an almost universally known symbol of personal failure, Willy Loman.

The activity of writing, then, is central to our professional roles as scholars. In this book we develop the view that the stories we discern in our field experiences as well as in the literature have to be authentically crafted and configured. We develop and theorize insights grounded in our field engagement, and offer them to particular audiences as representing something new and important to existing disciplinary thought. Only when these audiences have certified the work will our writing have made a contribution to the field.

OUR WRITING TASK

We now understand that the major task of writing our journals' texts involves working out how to convert our field engagement with people's conversations and lives into theoretically relevant insights and claims that are viewed as a contribution by the relevant professional community of readers. This under-standing recognizes that the texts we create using qualitative research require us to straddle and bring into dialectic relation two worlds, our academic disci-plinary community and the world of the group we studied. This writing task involves four components:

1. Articulating theoretically relevant insights gained from our field engage-ment with a particular social and cultural world. Contextualizing these insights in people's conversations, lived meanings, and events, orients the texts we write toward that world. At the same time, selecting and framing insights in theoretically relevant terms begins to turn the text back toward the academic disciplinary community to which we belong.

2. Identifying and shaping a contribution site as we connect these insights and extant literature in articulating knowledge claims. We will portray this work as a process of developing a theorized storyline, or plot, for our work that connects the academic and field worlds, and creates a particular theoretical space to which our study will contribute.

3. Authoritatively arguing the uniqueness and value of our theorized storyline by highlighting the literature's limitations and showing how our study addresses those limitations. We marshal our scholarship and particular research insights to persuade our audience that we have something new to add to existing disciplinary writing. In journal articles, we usually have the oppor-tunity to make one major extension or revision to extant literature.

4. Characterizing ourselves as academic storytellers who are members of the professional community in good standing. Hence, we attend to explicating

our methodology, appropriately referencing, and so on. We may also make choices in our writing that further characterize us as individual writers, such as type of argument we fashion, word selection, and so on. In our writing, then, we not only are constrained by the conventions of academic style, but also can shape that style through injection of a personal style.

And we do all of this with our words.

TWO

CRAFTING A THEORIZED
STORYLINE

⊹⦿⊹

How, then, do we go about this writing task? How do we bring together the academic and field worlds to develop theoretically relevant insights regarded as a contribution by disciplinary readers?

As noted earlier, stories provide a narrative structure for our work that arranges events and ideas according to some temporal sequencing of past, present and future. We have found it helpful to imagine our articles as nonfiction short stories that, like our articles, are based on true events and are developed to fit into a small number of pages. In a small space, and with attention to portraying truth, nonfiction short stories bring together events and efforts so that they cohere, or express some wholeness. Meaningfully connecting these events is the work of a plot, or storyline, often structured as complication, development and resolution (Franklin, 1994). Complication involves problems encountered by a person (or people) that matter or are troublesome; development concerns peoples' efforts and actions, and any twists and turns that flow from addressing a complication; and resolution concerns some sort of change in the person or situation that can be regarded as positive or negative, and that addresses a complication and may reduce tension. Stories that resonate more deeply with readers are those in which real people are confronted with significant problems, and, in their journey toward resolving the problem, those real people are profoundly changed (Franklin, 1994).

Applying a narrative perspective to the writing of disciplinary journal articles highlights the importance of crafting a *theorized storyline;* our writing efforts are necessarily directed to converting our field engagement into theoretical insights and ideas of interest and import to a disciplinary audience. By theorized storylines, then, we mean the articulation of a plot that relates the field and academic worlds via "literature-based" ideas that cohere with our field engagement. An example of a theorized storyline might read as follows:

> "Y" is an important phenomenon. The extant literature thinks "x" about "y." However, "y" is in reality more complicated than "x" suggests; "x" is not the whole story. This richer view of "y" is important because . . . Our study helps us to gain insight into what needs to be incorporated into the understanding of "y." If we adopt these theoretically relevant insights, we can better explain "y" or see it differently from before.

Gaining a sense of our field insights (field complication) challenges our prior thinking about "y." "X" is not the whole story of "y" (literature complication). Using the insights from the study to address this gap (development), we introduce a richer view of "y" (resolution).

For researchers using qualitative data, especially those having experienced intensive field engagement, crafting a theorized storyline is a difficult and time-consuming endeavor. We lament that although creating such storylines for journal publication brings disciplinary credibility and visibility to the work, the price exacted is serious compression of field engagement. Even though qualitative data and the field stories we construct from them express the richness and complexity of real-life interactions and events, their theoretical multivocality is in many ways inconsistent with the given journal-length paper in which we are generally able to articulate one storyline. Consequently, we need to craft storylines that draw on the theoretically relevant insights of field engagement and cultivate the optimal space for our work to contribute to the literature—all the while illuminating rather than silencing our field insights. In this chapter, we focus on the introductions of our journal articles to examine how authors variously set up these theorized storylines and secure readers' attention.

ESTABLISHING THEORIZED STORYLINES

As prior work has demonstrated (Bazerman, 1993; Golden-Biddle & Locke, 1993; Knorr-Cetina, 1981; Locke & Golden-Biddle, 1997; Swales & Najjar, 1987), it is in the introductions of journal articles that authors offer readers plausible proposals of knowledge for their consideration. It is here that establishing theorized storylines takes center stage. Integrating the work of Swales and Najjar (1987) with our own (Golden-Biddle & Locke, 1993; Locke & Golden-Biddle, 1997), we offer the following rhetorical moves that authors use to establish theorized storylines early in manuscripts:

1. Articulate study significance

2. Situate study in literature

3. Problematize literature to make space for study to contribute

4. Foreshadow how the present study addresses problematization

These moves are closely related, often developed in the same paragraph or even sentence. Together, they constitute the introduction; a central location in the manuscript designated for "managing relevances" for the study and "providing criteria of relevance according to which some results presented can be seen as more important than others" (Knorr-Cetina, 1981, p. 110).

MOVE 1: ARTICULATE STUDY SIGNIFICANCE

The first move articulates the significance of the study and more generally, the article by contextualizing it. Following the *Oxford English Dictionary,* we define *significance* as import or meaning. Thus, this first move creates the broadest relevance—import—for the article by contextualizing it in a more general world, whether that is everyday life or the literature.

The first two examples articulate significance by framing their studies as concerning ubiquitous and essential organizational phenomena whose under-standing will be enhanced by the research. The article by Jorgen Sandberg (2000) connects his study of human competence with commonplace and important organizational actions. He signals relevance through the use of particular phrases associated with competence.

> Organizational actions such as producing cars, treating illness, transporting, and educating are *always based* on human competence. A *fundamental managerial problem* is to develop human competence at work in a way that enables an organization to remain viable. Today, developing competence is also becoming an *increasingly important issue.* . . . However, in order to manage training and development efficiently, managers need to understand what constitutes human competence at work . . . (p. 9)

The second example, by Kevin Corley and Denny Gioia (2004), connects the ubiquitous phenomenon of change with their study of identity ambiguities, and signals relevance by conveying what it is like to experience identity ambiguity.

> Change is challenging. With any organizational change come unknowns. With unknowns come ambiguities. When those ambiguities concern the identity of the organization itself, it becomes *difficult for members* to make sense of "who we are as an organization," especially when traditional referents for understanding that identity lose their relevance. Ambiguity about identity is *uncomfortable,* at both the individual and organizational levels, and most would like to resolve it quickly to achieve some renewed semblance of clarity about their identity. . . . Some identity changes . . . are so sweeping and discontinuous that they *disrupt the order* of the understood world. One such occurrence is the spin-off of one organizational entity from its parent. . . . We know little about identity change in this context, which prompted our guiding research question: How does organizational identity change occur during a corporate spin-off? (pp. 173–175)

The next three examples articulate significance by contextualizing their studies in recognizable difficulties or complications being experienced by actors. In the first example, by William Miller, Benjamin Crabtree, Reuben McDaniel, and Kurt Stange (1998), we see physicians being "pushed to change" while simultaneously trying to "preserve their commitment to the . . . doctor–patient relationship. . . ." Relevance for their study of change in primary care practice is signaled through the use of words such as *turbulent, difficult, sacredness, virtues, pushed, essential.*

> These are turbulent and difficult times for primary care physicians and practices. Physicians are being asked to preserve their commitment to the sacredness of the doctor–patient relationship and the virtues of trust, fidelity, beneficence, and nonmaleficence. At the same time, they are being pushed to change the way they organize and deliver care and to alter and adjust to specific skills, knowledge, and style of practice they use. Attempts to introduce change by policymakers, administrators, and researchers have been rejected or implemented in unanticipated ways or with unforeseen consequences. Yet, some practices do seek and create change with minimum or no help, and there is the occasional change that is adopted by many practices. Understanding the organization of primary care practices is essential for the determination of how changes in the delivery of preventive or other health care services are implemented. This article reviews the literature on changing

practice behavior, presents case studies of primary care practice and then introduces a conceptual model . . . for a better understanding of practice organization. (p. 369)

In the second example, by Jean-Louis Denis, Ann Langley, and Marc Pineault (2000), we see new CEOs "entering, understanding and mastering a new organization" in the face of strong and particular performance expectations. Relevance for their study of leader entry is signaled through juxtaposing typical expectations of a new CEO with prevailing entry dynamics.

> The "romantic conception" of the chief executive officer (CEO) as the *all-powerful, all-knowing, controller* of the destiny of a complex enterprise persists in the business press (Meindl et al., 1985). Moreover, the expectation often seems to be that within a few months of his or her arrival, a new CEO will have diagnosed the organization's strengths and weaknesses, enunciated new strategic visions, proposed plans for restructuring, and more generally be "*in control*" (e.g. Dobrzynski, 1993). *Yet, the process of entering, understanding and mastering a new organization is far from simple* . . . our research aimed to develop an understanding of the dynamics of the entry process . . . (pp. 1063–1064)

And in the third example, by Jane Dutton, Monica Worline, Peter Frost, and Jacoba Lilius (2006), readers are drawn into the inevitability of experiencing pain and suffering. Relevance for their study of compassion organizing is further signaled by the listing of specific life conditions in which pain is experienced.

> Pain and suffering are an *inevitable part of the lived experience* of all organizational members (Frost, 2003). Pain can arise from life conditions, such as *illness, family strife, and loss, or stem from work experiences like poor treatment, accidents, layoffs, or thwarted aspirations*. While events and conditions that occasion pain for organizational members are limitless, there are real limits to organizational researchers' understanding of how such pain occasions the activation and mobilization of collective responding. This paper addresses the gap in organization researchers' knowledge around how responses to pain are coordinated and patterned into a form of organizing.

The final two examples articulate significance by contextualizing and then immediately challenging the study and experience of everyday phenomena. In these examples, the move of articulating significance is closely related to the third move, which problematizes a literature to create space for the study's contribution. But these articles cast a broader relevance net. The first example, by Joanne Martin, Kathleen Knopoff, and Christine Beckman (1998), challenges both organizational theory and life in organizations for overlooking the subject of emotions. This challenge is set up in the opening sentence through a comparison, created in the use of the conjunction, *yet,* and the juxtaposition between people's constant experience of emotions and the *largely deemphasized, marginalized* or *ignored* exploration of those emotions in life or theory.

> People constantly experience emotions, yet in organizational theory, as in organizational life, the exploration of emotions has been largely deemphasized, marginalized, or ignored. Impersonal criteria for making decisions and restraints on emotional expression at work have long been the hallmarks of bureaucracy (e.g. Weber, 1946, 1981). Recent work has broken this emotional taboo, exploring how certain organizations require the expression of particular emotions at work to maximize organizational productivity, an aspect of work that has been labeled emotional labor (Hochschild, 1983). . . .
> In contrast, feminist organizational theorists have taken a focus on emotions one step closer to a kind of personal authenticity, arguing that expression of a wider range of emotions at work (labeled bounded emotionality) is desirable, not to enhance productivity but to foster the psychological well-being of organizational members and their families (Mumby & Putnam, 1992; Putnam & Mumby, 1993; Meyerson, 1998). . . . This paper focuses on . . . the management of emotion, and asks whether it is possible for a large organization . . . to find new ways of integrating emotional expression into organizational life . . . is the isomorphism of bureaucracy in an iron cage, or is it possible to find ways of doing business differently, on a large scale? (pp. 429–430)

The second example, by Jennifer Howard-Grenville (2005), challenges contradictory findings in organizational theory: on the one hand, routines have *traditionally been seen as* a source of inertia and on the other, *recent work* shows routines as a source of change. This challenge is set up through the immediate use of two questions in the opening paragraph, which also cast the relevance net for this study: *Or do they?* And *How do we explain these apparent contradictions?*

> Routines are central to organizing (March & Simon, 1958; Cyert & March, 1963; Feldman & Pentland, 2003), so central, in fact, that routines explain the behavior of firms (Nelson & Winter, 1982: 128). Or do they? Routines

have traditionally been seen as a source of organizational inertia, and their intentional recombination a source of organizational adaptation (Cyert & March, 1963; Nelson & Winter, 1982). But recent work also demonstrates the opposite: the everyday use of routines can bring about change (Feldman, 2000; Feldman & Pentland, 2003) and the intentional alteration of routines can result in no change (Edmondson, Bohmer & Pisano, 2001; Feldman, 2003). How do we explain these apparent contradictions? . . . In this paper, I use data from a nine month ethnographic study of a high-tech manufacturing organization, Chipco, to build theory on the persistence and change of flexible, task-oriented routines. (pp. 618–619)

In exploring the first rhetorical move, we have shown how articles articulate significance through their placement in relation with something else. Significance requires contextualization. Our examples, by no means exhaustive, have illustrated contexts of essential organizational phenomena, recognizable difficulties or complications experienced by some actors or those associated with everyday phenomena.

The second and third rhetorical moves are developed from our study (Locke & Golden-Biddle, 1997) of the construction of contribution in journal articles. In the second move of situating the study in the literature, the articles re-present and organize existing knowledge. The articles variously construe the extant literature as synthesized, progressive and noncoherent. In the third move, problematizing the literature, the articles subvert the very literature that they just constructed by identifying a problem variously construed as a gap, an oversight, or a misdirection. We did not find a one-to-one correspondence between the moves of constructing and problematizing the literature in light of the study. Instead, any of the three ways of constructing the literature could be, and was, connected with any of the three ways of problematizing that literature. Thus, we found nine different ways in which the literature base of the theorized storyline was crafted.

MOVE 2: SITUATE STUDY IN LITERATURE

The second move is accomplished via the active selection and shaping of literature to be joined. In our study, we called this process constructing intertextual coherence. It concerns how the article configures and references the relationship among extant work, and between extant work and the proposed study. We regard writing the "lit review" to be a major task in the crafting of theorized storylines. Consider, for a moment, where we go to find out about a topic; there is no pre-given depository under a "subject" index. There are as many versions of what "the literature" in a given area comprises as there are people writing and reading in that area. To be sure, there is significant overlap, and theorists may agree on what constitute key works in a theoretical domain, but even that is not guaranteed. Certainly, there is not a one-to-one agreement on all the works relevant to a topic under investigation.

Consider further that what constitutes the "body of knowledge" is not fixed once and for all by the publication of work. This is a reality with which anyone who has had their work cited is acquainted! Other readers with different understandings of the area or different interests may draw different conclusions and points from the work. Thus, a particular work may be disparately relevant to various readers who selectively draw specific aspects of the work.

When we write up our discussion of extant literature, we are doing much more than generating a summary of previous studies and theorizing on a topic. We construct existing knowledge in a way that makes room for our research and invites the contribution our work can make. It is as if we configure and reassemble the available pieces of a jigsaw puzzle in such a way that they contour an opening or a space into which our theorized storyline will fit. We rewrite existing work to illuminate the contribution made by our study.

To illustrate, Karen Locke (1996) located the contribution of her study on physician–patient interactions in two literatures: organizational emotions and service encounters. To do this, her presentation of related works and relevant citations needed to materialize an intersection between the two research streams.

> The literatures on organizational emotions and service management have an overlapping interest in the affect that occurs in face-to-face encounters between service providers and consumers. For example, much research on organizational emotions has focused on the display of positive feelings by employees who hold boundary spanning positions in service encounters (Ash, 1984; Hochschild, 1983; Peters & Waterman, 1983; Peven, 1968; Sutton & Rafaeli, 1988; Van Maanen & Kunda, 1989). While, in the service management literature, the display of positive emotions is viewed as central to service providers' roles (Czepiel, Solomon, & Suprenant, 1985; Suprenant & Solomon,1987) and to the formation of consumer satisfaction (Czepiel et al. 1985; Oliver, 1995; Parsuraman, Zeithaml, & Berry, 1985) . . . (p. 40)

The point of intersection is created by rewriting the literature on organizational emotions to underscore its attention to service encounters and, conversely, by rewriting the service encounter literature to emphasize its concern with emotions. Writing each literature to highlight something that they had in common, then, constituted a flexible use of them as a resource.

Martin Kilduff's (1993) analysis of *Organizations* indicates that March and Simon (1958) conveniently left out of their discussion of the literature at least two major works that were inconsistent with their indictment of organizational research as subscribing to a machine-like view of human beings. This selectivity allowed them to intensify and press home the predominance of the mechanistic model, and set up their own theorizing as a much needed, new perspective. In a different discipline, evolutionary biology, Bazerman (1993) demonstrates the partiality in Stephen J. Gould and Richard Lewontin's (1979) characterization of their literature. In this article, Gould and Lewontin seek to discredit the "adaptationist programme," a broad theoretical framework proposing an adaptive explanation of the survival value of every physical and behavioral feature of a species. To serve their enterprise and highlight the contribution their work makes, they construct the existing literature in evolutionary biology as a struggle between "foolish adaptationism and a wiser pluralism" (Bazerman, 1993, p. 37).

Our point is not that scholars misrepresent the literature to advance their own arguments. Rather, our point is that there is sufficient fluidity and ambiguity in any topical literature to allow it to be authentically interpreted and shaped in a number of directions. Certainly, there are outer limits and norms for constructing literature. But within those limits, there is flexibility in the use of prior knowledge (Golden-Biddle, Locke, & Reay, 2006). When we examined how literatures are constructed in the introductions of articles, we discerned three ways: synthesized coherence, progressive coherence and noncoherence.

Synthesized Coherence

This construction of the literature involves putting together work that previously had been considered unrelated. It highlights the need for new work, for example, the present study, by disclosing an undeveloped investigative concern that is common to the referenced work. Studies that might otherwise be viewed as unrelated are connected by constructing congruent relationships among the different referenced research streams and studies.

Articles construct synthesized coherence in two typical ways. The first one involves the organization of quite discrepant references. In this regard, articles have characterized their intertextual fields as reporting *"bits and pieces* of evidence" on how organizations try to maintain the expression of desirable emotions in light of actors' inner feelings (Sutton, 1991, p. 246), or containing the *"building blocks* for a process model of organizational death . . . in writings on organizational growth and in the sparse literature on dying organizations" (Sutton & Callahan, 1987, p. 542).

The second one creates intersections between two or more acknowledged but distinct research programs. The writing of connection between these programs is evident in comments such as, *"despite discrepant pragmatic aims,* and regardless of nuances in definition, organizational theorists who write about organizational cultures repeatedly employ key terms that bear a *family resemblance"* (Barley, 1983, p. 393), and in suggestions that studies of culture are *"intellectually akin* to a simultaneously growing literature" on organizational symbolism (p. 393). Additional examples of connecting diverse literatures include construing commonality between family theorists and organizational theorists (Hirschhorn & Gilmore, 1980), or relating the work of authors who studied different topics, but which, "nevertheless are of considerable interest to the student of intermediary organizations" (Lammers, 1988).

Progressive Coherence

In contrast to synthesized coherence, which relates disparate works containing as yet undisclosed points of intersection, progressive coherence incorporates works already recognized as related in theoretical perspectives and methods. A construction of progressive coherence depicts cumulative knowledge growth over time and consensus among researchers in a well-developed and focused line of inquiry.

Lynn Isabella's (1990) presentation of the literature on the process of organizational change offers an example of progressive coherence. Look at how she writes the literature as gradually filtering toward a need to understand managers' interpretive processes:

> Within the literature on organizational change, there has been considerable research on the sequence of activities that facilitates the process of change (Delbecq & Van de Ven, 1971; Hage & Aiken, 1970; Lewin, 1947; Lippit, Watson & Westley, 1958). Although change at its most basic level has been said to consist of unfreezing, moving and refreezing (Lewin, 1947), movement through these stages involves more than sequential activities and behaviors. Recent research on selected changes (e.g. Bartunek, 1984; Gephart,

1984; Sutton, 1987) and the literature on organizational change in general have suggested that a substantial amount of cognition and interpretation accompanies the process of change. In other words, as a change unfolds, different assumptions and orientations are required at different times in the process. Managers involved in a change need to undergo an alteration of their cognitive structure (Benne, 1976) that facilitates and supports the need to change, the process of changing, and the maintenance of what has been changed. The frame of reference—the perspective through which people view an event—shifts (McCall, 1977; Starbuck, 1976).

The text begins with citations that document an interest in the sequence of activities that advance change. It moves next to work indicating that managers' cognitive processes and interpretive behaviors play a key role in moving through the change process. It ends with a concern for understanding managers' frames of reference. The literature is written as a set-up for the present article, which explicates as a logical next step the study of "the precise nature of these different and changing managerial cognitions and interpretations" (Isabella, 1990, p. 8).

The achievement of cumulative progress is often portrayed through the use of multiple citations. For example, density of citations coupled with descriptors of the literature underscore that significant research efforts have been devoted to a topic, as illustrated in the article by Julianne Cheek and Terri Gibson (2003, p. 134),

> A *considerable body of international literature* provides evidence that hospitalization can have adverse effects on older people (Wilkinson and Sainsbury, 1998; Davis et al, 1999; Jacelon, 1999).

Or, in Ng and De Cock's (2002, p. 24) study of a battle in the boardroom of a Singapore company,

> We take a distinctive position which locates us *alongside a range of other writers* who are interested in narrative as a way of expressing practical knowledge and understanding organizational processes (Barrett et al, 1995; Czarniawska, 1997; Keenoy et al, 1997; Rhodes, 2000; Watson & Harris, 1999).

Serializing the citations also connotes cumulative progress by showing how successive cohorts of researchers have contributed to a topic, as illustrated by the following example (Bechky, 2003, p. 312),

Much of the research that conceptualizes these challenges [of integrating understandings of different groups across organizations] has emphasized general processes that organizations use to codify and transfer knowledge from localized contexts (March & Simon 1958, Levitt & March 1988, Huber 1991, Cohen & Bacdayan 1994). . . . *Other scholars* have observed that successful knowledge transfer is not so simple, and emphasize that the tacitness of much knowledge often makes codification, transfer and subsequent replication of routines and standard operating procedures difficult (Nonaka 1991, 1994; Nelson & Winter 1982; Kogut & Zander 1992).

Successive cohorts are shown as contributing to a growing understanding of challenges associated with integrating different group's understandings across an organization.

Noncoherence

In articles constructing noncoherent intertextual fields, we find referenced works presented as belonging to a common research program, but which are now linked by disagreement. In contrast to the previous two ways of constructing literature in which consensus is figural, here the focus is on the construction of discord, though nevertheless discord among researchers who agree on the importance of the research domain.

Two examples illustrate the construction of noncoherent intertextual fields that characterize the field in terms of contention. The first example (Langton, 1984, p. 330) claims that "unfortunately, the relevant literature offers *contradictory assessments* and the second (Yan & Gray, 1994, p. 1479) refers to "*continuing controversy* in the international joint venture literature." In each example, this dissensus also extends to researchers working within the same research program.

On the one hand, we are told that "Max Weber was the first to consider bureaucracy as the problem of industrial society" (Jacoby, 1973:147), that he articulated the "Classical theory of bureaucracy" (Blau, 1970:14) and that this theory, "despite substantial modification and revision, remains the dominant paradigm for the study of administration and formal organization" (Rudolph & Rudolph, 1979:195; Ouchi, 1980:401–402). All this clearly conveys the impression that Weber's views on bureaucracy constitutes as Landau (1972:154) explicitly argued, "a paradigm in Kuhn's sense." *On the other hand, this same literature contends* that all theories of bureaucracy, including Weber's, are "underdeveloped" (Heiskanen, quoted in Abrahamsson, 1977:36.). (from Langton, 1984, p. 330)

> Research findings on the relationship between control and performance offer *conflicting results* (see Geringer and Hebert (1984) for a review). (from Yan & Gray, 1994, p. 1479)

Throughout articles constructing noncoherence, we find phrases like those in the above excerpts, *contradictory assessments* and *continuing controversy.* Additional examples include *no consensus* (Holm, 1995), *competing explanations* (Bills, 1987), *echoes this confusion* (Perlow, Okhuysen, & Repenning, 2002) and *depressing disputes* (Riley, 1983). Other examples include depictions of researchers as pitted against each other. Thus, Connie Gersick's (1994) text constructs *opposing camps* of researchers on the organizational adaptability issue, locating a group of researchers in each camp. Her earlier work (1988, p. 11) also writes in such challenges by noting that "Bell (1982) and Seeger (1983) *questioned* Bales and Strodtbeck's methodology, too." And finally, Bills's (1987) portrayal of three disparate perspectives, "*one stream* of thought . . . *Other writers* . . . Osterman is quite convinced that *neither interpretation* is entirely satisfactory" points to a research program in disarray.

In the second rhetorical move, we have shown how articles variously situate studies in constructing extant literature as synthesized coherence, progressive coherence or noncoherence. Although establishing theorized storylines relies on situating studies in literature, we have seen that such constructions are by no means simply received. Rather, how we construct the literature not only shapes and delimits, but also creates an important resource in discerning potential storylines.

MOVE 3: PROBLEMATIZE LITERATURE TO MAKE SPACE FOR STUDY TO CONTRIBUTE

The third move in establishing theorized storylines both relies on and calls into question the intertextual field developed in the second move. In subverting the very literature just constructed, the article creates a gap that enables it to argue the uniqueness and value of the theorized storyline authoritatively. We marshal our scholarship and theoretically relevant field insights to persuade our audience that there is something lacking in existing disciplinary writing. Without this gap or lacunae, the scientific version of a literary trope (Gephart, 1986, p. 2004), there is no room for the study to make a contribution; there is no means by which "y" can be viewed differently before and after the study. In journal articles, we usually have the opportunity to make one major extension or revision to extant literature.

Rather than disclosing a uniform way to problematize extant literature, our study (Locke & Golden-Biddle, 1997) found three ways to construct a gap: extant literature as incomplete, inadequate, and incommensurate. Seen as a continuum, as we move across from incomplete through inadequate and on to incommensurate, we find increasing negation and upheaval of that constructed literature.

Incomplete

The hallmark of an incomplete problematization is the identification of a gap by which the article claims that the extant literature is not fully finished; it seeks to contribute by specifying and filling in what is not finished. Following the storyline, the complication consists of identifying where further specification is needed in the structured intertextual field, and the resolution addresses that specification. Thus, articles problematizing the literature as incomplete seek to refine or further specify existing thinking, "x" about "y." Note how the following excerpt, which constructs the literature as "progressive coherence," identifies the gap as the unspecified aspect of how improvisation shapes learning (vs. extant work on how learning shapes improvisation).

> Work to date thus provides *ample evidence* that the construct of improvisation can generate lively discussion and that instances of improvisation are found in organizations. One recurring theme of both research and lay observations is that stored knowledge and skills shape improvisation in important ways. . . . *At the core of prior work is the argument* that the result of prior learning, organizational memory, shapes the skillful and fruitful improvisation of novel performances. *Research is less clear, however, about whether and how improvisation affects learning,* focusing instead on the outcomes of improvisation itself, such as saved firefighters or firms. We wondered whether improvisation would result in a different set of behaviors or insights relative to what firms would have experienced under normal planning and execution. (from Miner, Bassoff, & Moorman, 2001, pp. 304–305)

An example from Kathy Kram and Lynn Isabella (1985), excerpted below, illustrates the identification of a gap in extant literature requiring greater specification. Situated in the mentoring literature, the text complicates this literature by incorporating the notion of "*other* adult relationships," implying that mentoring relationships are but one type of relationship in work settings important for individual growth. The text fully specifies the gap in one sentence near the end of the introduction and through the use of the conjunction, *yet*.

Yet, while we know the general importance of relationships, we know little about adult relationships other than the mentoring relationship that directly encourage, support, and contribute to progress in life and career. (p. 122)

Inadequate

Illuminating oversights is the hallmark of texts that problematize the field as "inadequate." These texts claim that extant literature does not sufficiently incorporate different perspectives and alternative views of the phenomena under investigation. That is, extant work has overlooked perspectives relevant and important to better understanding and explaining phenomena. The article clears a space to contribute by pointing out the oversight and introducing an alternative perspective or framework. This problematization stops short, however, of advocating that the extant intertextual field is wrong, preferring instead to allow the proposed alternative framework to coexist with those in extant work.

In establishing this type of problematization, authors seek to augment extant thought. Thus, the construction of the theorized storyline goes something like this: "In the beginning, the organization studies literature thought 'x' about 'y.' However, 'x' is not the whole story about 'y.' Particular elements such as 'a,' 'b,' and 'c' have been left out. Based on this field study, here are our claims to knowledge about 'y.' By adopting these insights, we can better explain the whole story about 'y.'"

The article by Abhijit Gopal and Pushkala Prasad (2000) sets up an inadequate problematization of extant work on group decision support systems in the information technology literature. In particular, they accomplish this problematization through questioning whether this work has "achieved the credibility it needs to serve as a blueprint for future research," ascertaining it has not, and suggesting that the goal of striving for "consistent and positive results" "might need to be reexamined."

As in many of the "interest areas" defined within the rubric of information technology (IT), the research literature on group decision support systems (GDSS) has burgeoned over a period of about a decade and a half, working hard to make sense of the use and misuse of group-oriented information systems . . .

It is important, however, to pause at this juncture and ask whether GDSS scholarship to date has achieved the credibility it needs to serve as a blueprint for future research, especially on influential technologies such as enterprise resource planning (ERP) systems, which put IT on an entirely different footing in organizations. . . . At first glance, the pan-organizational focus of

GDSS would suggest that this might be feasible. But has GDSS established an adequate track record? Has it come close to achieving its own implicit goals of establishing some level of unambiguous knowledge about GDSS and its effects? A glance at the GDSS literature over the last decade appears to suggest that such might not be the case. There is wide acknowledgement that research results have been either inconsistent or non-existent . . . there is increasing complexity. . . . And there appears to be little accord among researchers on theory, method or relevance to practice . . .

The solutions proposed, unfortunately, have resulted in the proliferation of theories and methods and in the fragmentation of views within the community. . . . *What has remained stable throughout, however, is the scientific (Dennis et al 1999) drive for consistent and "positive" (i.e. pro-GDSS) results. In view of the varying results to date and the wide range of circumstances under which such systems are called into use, this goal itself might need to be reexamined. Is it clear that consistent, positive results are actually possible? We believe it is not* and it is our purpose in this paper to attempt to establish this position . . .

The next excerpt, which constructs the literature as synthesized coherence, develops an inadequate problematization by suggesting that current research on board functioning overlooks cultural elements. This problematization makes space for the study's findings concerning organizational identity to expand extant thinking about board functioning.

Although there is . . . work on how the functioning of boards is shaped by structural connections . . . political activism . . . and cognitive biases . . . there is *no empirical work on how it is influenced by the cultural context.* In this paper, we seek to illuminate the cultural embeddedness of boards by examining . . . 1) How does a hybrid organizational identity shape the way board members define themselves, and construct their role? 2) What do board members do when a crisis makes hitherto latent contradictions in organizational identity visible? . . . Our analyses disclose that identity shapes the board role and . . . when a crisis punctures . . . expectations of that role, conflicts of commitment emerge that threaten governance . . . (from Golden-Biddle & Rao, 1997)

An additional example below, which constructs the literature as progressive coherence, illustrates an inadequate problematization by claiming that research on creativity assessment has important "shortcomings."

To summarize, although it has been widely assumed that accurately assessing people's creative potential confers important organizational benefits, no research has systematically examined the specific judgmental processes organizational decision makers actually use when trying to assess such potential. Further, although there has been some research on creativity assessment in laboratory settings, the extent to which findings from these studies generalize to organizational assessments of creativity remains unclear. Together, these *shortcomings* in current theory and research *underline the lack of clear understanding of how expert decision makers assess others' creative potential in organizational settings.* (from Elsbach & Kramer, 2003, pp. 284–285)

One final example of an inadequate problematization is the excerpt from an article by David Thomas (1993). Consider, as you read, how it illuminates oversights.

In the past several years, race relations has continued to grow in importance as a topic of academic interest. It is now recognized that despite gains made since the 1960s, racial inequalities persist . . . Yet organizational research has rarely focused on the dynamics of interracial work-centered relationships and thus has offered little to advance our understanding of the influence of race on organizational processes. . . . Little research has been done on developmental relationships in racially integrated workplaces that examines how these relationships work. This paper addressed that issue . . . (pp. 169–170)

What is the theorized storyline proposed by Thomas? Before reading on, take a moment to frame what you perceive as his storyline.

To us, his storyline reads: In the past few years, the subject of race relations and research on race relations is increasing in importance "*as a topic of academic interest.*" However, important aspects on the subject have been left out of most studies. In particular, "*little research has been done on developmental relationships in racially integrated workplaces.*" This study's findings will provide a more comprehensive rendering of the influence of race relations in work organizations.

Incommensurate

The hallmark of articles that construct an "incommensurate" problematization is their direct advocacy for an alternative idea or thesis that is better than those put forth in extant literature. Whereas we need to look closely at articles with inadequate problematizations to discern partisanship, in those with incommensurate problematizations, partisanship is explicitly conveyed. Here, it is claimed that extant literature not only overlooks different and relevant perspectives, but it is wrong, misguided or incorrect.

In contrast to refining or augmenting the extant literature, articles that problematize the literature as incommensurate seek to reformulate or redirect that literature. The storyline goes something like this: "In the beginning, the organization studies literature thought 'x' about 'y.' However, 'x' is misleading, wrong, or significantly incomplete. Based on this field study, here's what should be said about 'y.' If we adopt these insights, we can redirect our thinking and better explain 'y.'" Note how the following three excerpts challenge extant literature.

We begin with an excerpt from the article by Beth Bechky (2003) that challenges extant work on knowledge transfer. Although close to an inadequate problematization, it approaches the realm of incommensurate problematization when it states that the assumptions of the *simple* knowledge transfer model do not just overlook a particular aspect or perspective, but *in practice,* [they] *do not hold.*

> Although this work has significantly enhanced our understanding of why knowledge management and integration is so difficult, it treats "knowledge" as a given. While theorists realize that the mechanical notion of knowledge transfer is a limited one, it *persists in our thinking* about knowledge in organizations, implying the communication of knowledge is a simple process (Reddy, 1979). Conceptualizing knowledge in organizations with the *impoverished metaphor* of knowledge transfer has several implications. *Simple* knowledge transfer assumes a referential theory of meaning and implies that within organizations, meaning is universal and context is relatively homogeneous. *Yet in practice, these assumptions do not hold* . . . (p. 313)

Arguing that stories examined in previous research on storytelling have been "*wrenched* from their natural performance contexts," the article by David Boje (1991) advocates for the alternative thesis that storytelling be studied as a dynamic process occurring within a performative context. Clearly, *wrench* is not a neutral word. Soon after, other literature and citations re-marshaled to support the alternative thesis. Concluding this section, just prior to the direct challenge, is the claim that these more "complex aspects of storytelling in organizations" have been "ignored" by organizational analyses of story.

Up to now, the problematization could be categorized as inadequate, though there are certainly clues to the developing incommensurate problematization. It still has the opportunity to construe an inadequate problematization:

in this case, the storytelling process in context is an alternative perspective that deserves to be studied and to be incorporated alongside other perspectives. However, in the very next sentence and the following 112 lines of the article, the direct challenge of extant literature on storytelling is made explicit.

> Stories in previous laboratory, history and questionnaire research generally have been wrenched from their natural performance contexts and treated as objectified social facts (Ritzer, 1975), mere texts, with little empirical attention given to the natural linguistic context in which the stories are being performed. Text research does not capture basic aspects of the situated language performance . . . In case history studies, researchers have relied on second- and third-hand accounts of a story, rather than examining a storytelling event in process . . . In the case of lab study research performance skills are not a consideration . . . the transition from the lab to the organization is fraught with difficulties . . . Story-text studies relying on interview methods have also ignored performance behavior . . . Finally, in the case of surveys, the textual content, rather than the storytelling event is the focus of study . . . Such an approach does not tell us about how those stories were performed in their natural elements . . . it is not a behavioral analysis of in situ performance . . . Stories can therefore be correctly interpreted only to the extent that the researcher grasps the story in situ . . . . (pp. 106–109)

Through the use of the word *wrench;* questions that challenge prior research results; the continual juxtaposition between prior research and the proposed alternative; and the insertion of the words *situated, real, in situ, natural, performance* and *context,* this text directly challenges extant literature, and advocates for its own, alternative thesis. It doesn't want to coexist with prior work; it wants to replace it with the proposed perspective. Finally, it pronounces that *Stories can therefore be correctly interpreted only to the extent that the researcher grasps the story in situ. . . .* The strong implication is, of course, that research conducted on stories out of context is incorrect.

Our final example of incommensurate problematization, the article by Kathleen Eisenhardt (1989), challenges traditional literature by suggesting that *extant views may inaccurately describe how executives make rapid decisions.* The article begins with a story of failed decision making in a context demanding speed, and indicates that this story is *not unusual,* but there has been *little research on fast strategic decision making.* Immediately thereafter, it identifies the study's proposed contribution: *This article explores the speed of strategic decision making. . . . The empirical grounding of those ideas is the subject of this article.* Sandwiched between these two neutral sentences stated in line with scientific norms (Knorr-Cetina, 1981; Gephart, 1988) is the essence of this text's incommensurate problematization, as follows:

> The results reported here are a set of propositions challenging traditional views of strategic decision making. The evidence suggests that fast decision makers *use more, not less,* information than do slow decision makers. They also *develop more, not fewer,* alternatives. In contrast to current literature, this study found that centralized decision making is not necessarily fast, but a layered advice process emphasizing input from experienced counselors, is fast. The findings also indicate that conflict resolution is critical to decision speed, but conflict per se is not. Finally, integration among strategic decisions and between decisions and tactical plans *speeds, not slows,* decision making. Such integration helps decision makers cope with the anxiety of high-stakes decision making. Overall, fast decision making allows decision makers to keep pace with change and is linked to strong performance. (Eisenhardt, 1989, p. 544)

Although the challenge is cast politely, through the constant juxtapositioning of prior research and this study's findings—a linguistic device prevalent in this problematization of the literature—this article provocates and advocates for its own thesis that executive teams make rapid decisions differently from what the literature would presuppose.

MOVE 4: FORESHADOW HOW THE PRESENT STUDY ADDRESSES PROBLEMATIZATION

In the first three moves, the text has cleared the way for the present study to make a contribution to the literature. In articulating significance, situating the study in a construction of extant literature and problematizing that very literature, the scene is set for the study to foreshadow how it intends to address the gap in this significant area. Thus, this fourth and final move is accomplished via the insertion of the study into the space created by the earlier moves. It specifies how the present research intends to occupy this space and is rhetorically accomplished by a turn toward the present study. As Swales and Najjar (1987) explain, "In Move 4, the *gap* is turned into the research space for the present article, or an offer is made to answer the question raised in Move 3" (p. 179).

The first example portrays a complication faced by physicians who need to deal with change and preserve their commitment to the doctor–patient relationship. Space is created for this study of change in the primary care practice organization through the last three sentences, beginning with the use of the word *yet,* indicating that change is a real possibility.

> These are turbulent and difficult times for primary care physicians and practices. Physicians are being asked to preserve their commitment to the sacredness of the doctor–patient relationship and the virtues of trust, fidelity, beneficence, and nonmaleficence . . . Attempts to introduce change by policymakers, administrators, and researchers have been rejected or implemented in unanticipated ways or with unforeseen consequences. *Yet,* some practices do seek and create change with minimum or no help, and there is the occasional change that is adopted by many practices. Understanding the organization of primary care practices is essential for the determination of how changes in the delivery of preventive or other health care services are implemented. *This article reviews the literature on changing practice behavior, presents case studies of primary care practice and then introduces a conceptual model . . . for a better understanding of practice organization.* (from Miller, Crabtree, McDaniel, & Stange, 1998, p. 369)

The second example, a study of agency and context in the performance of routines (Howard-Grenville, 2005), constructs a progressive coherence of the literature and an inadequate problematization: *While we know a great deal about . . . routines . . . we know much less about . . . how the people enacting a routine and the context . . . influence both a routine's use . . . and its change or persistence.* To turn this problematization into research space for the study to contribute, the article indicates that "what we know less about" are its "key concerns" and that this study, in particular examination of the "roadmapping" routine, will help "build theory" in this area.

> While we know a great deal about a wide variety of routines in a wide variety of organizational settings (Gersick & Hackman, 1990; Adler, Goldoftas & Levine, 1999; Weick, Sutcliffe & Obstfeld, 1999; Feldman, 2000; Narduzzo, Rocco & Warglien, 2000; Edmonson, Bohmer & Pisano, 2001) we know much less about how the people enacting a routine and the context in which it is enacted influence both a routine's use at a given point in time and its change or persistence over time. *These are the key concerns of this paper. In this paper, I use data from a nine month ethnographic study of a high-tech manufacturing organization, Chipco, to build theory on the persistence and change of flexible, task-oriented routines . . .* Central to Chipco's technology development practices, "roadmapping" was a pervasive, persistent organizational routine that nonetheless, on close inspection, admitted a lot of variation . . .

The last example, from an article by Wanda Orlikowski (2002), constructs
the literature on knowledge as progressive coherence and then problematizes
it as inadequate in its treatment of knowledge. In the excerpt below, research
space is created for the study to contribute by suggesting that an alternate view
of "knowing as enacted in practice"—and the "central role for practices"
accorded by this view—helps to better understand "competence generation" as
well as a "range of [other] organizational activities":

> Existing approaches to studying distributed organizing tend to focus on the
> importance of knowledge transfer across boundaries, and the value of gener-
> ating a set of "best practices" that can be propagated through the dispersed
> operations. A view of knowing as enacted in practice does not view compe-
> tence as something to be "transferred," and suggests that the very notion of
> "best practices" is problematic. When practices are defined as the situated
> recurrent activities of human agents, they cannot simply be spread around as
> if they were fixed and static objects. Rather, competence generation may be
> seen to be a process of developing people's capacity to enact what we may
> term "useful practices"—with usefulness seen to be a necessarily contextual
> and provisional aspect of situated organizational activity.
>
> *In the research study described below*, I explore the globally dispersed,
> product development work of a large and successful multinational organiza-
> tion (Kappa). The empirical insights suggest a central role for practices that
> produce and sustain a collective and distributed knowing within the global
> organization. *Such a focus on practices has not been central to current
> research on either global product development or organizational knowledge.
> Because it may be a valuable perspective for understanding a range of orga-
> nizational activities, it is the focus of my attention here.* (pp. 253–254)

How do we bring together academic and field worlds to develop theoretically relevant insights regarded as a contribution by disciplinary readers? How
do we accomplish this in writing journal articles in our disciplinary communities? We have suggested that we craft theorized storylines, or plots that weave
together relevant literature with our field insights. Such crafting is constituted
in four rhetorical moves: articulating the study's significance; situating the
study in a literature constructed as synthesized coherence, progressive coherence, or noncoherence; problematizing that literature to create a gap, and turn-
ing the gap into a space of contribution for the study. In the next chapter, we
examine how authors variously develop these theorized storylines through
engaging the fieldwork in their writing.

⊰ THREE ⊱

DEVELOPING THE
THEORIZED STORYLINE

———◆———

One of the hallmarks of qualitative research is the mounds of data, often comprised of hundreds and thousands of pages, produced from having gone *in* to organizations to learn about them. Made possible by extended stays in the field—often lasting a year, or even longer, in research programs—we are able to see first hand the everyday complexities and on-the-ground efforts for resolution associated with issues such as introducing and implementing technologies (Orlikowski, 1993; Trauth & Jessup, 2000), working collaboratively in virtual teams whose members are spread across the globe (Sarker & Sahay, 2004), interacting with family members in emergency rooms during resuscitation (Morse & Pooler, 2002), entering an occupation (Pratt, Rockmann, & Kaufmann, 2006; Ibarra, 1999; Van Maanen & Schein, 1979), providing care to older people in acute care settings (Cheek & Gibson, 2003), coping with disasters (Gephart, 1988, 1993; Turner, 1976; Vaughan, 1990; Weick, 1988, 1993), and so on. As a result, we are able to produce thick descriptions of everyday life in these contexts that also can enrich our theories and vitalize our theorized storylines.

But, how do we represent these vast data in developing our theorized storylines for journal articles that are constrained by space limitations? And how do we do this in a way that engages readers in our stories? Facing this dilemma, authors' efforts to compose qualitative research for journal articles have produced some innovation in representation. It is no longer the case, for example, that "findings" must be contained in a single section with that heading. Nor is it the case that all data must be depicted in tables (although it is increasingly common for additional qualitative data to support claims to be rendered in this form). No longer are theoretical models placed only at the fronts of papers. In this chapter, we explore four representational innovations, and the various solutions derived, that qualitative researchers have undertaken in their efforts of writing for disciplinary journals.

COMPELLING BEGINNINGS

Opening lines and sections are crucial elements in the establishment of rapport between the work and its readers (Law & Williams, 1982). In journal articles, the conventional "Abstract" remains. But, rather than simply stating what will follow in the article, some authors are writing "the first sentence so the readers want to read the second" (Fine, 1988, p. 156). As authors, when we consider *how* we write and how we represent our fieldwork in our writing, we are able to construct more compelling beginnings for our journal articles.

Some authors are choosing to take readers immediately to the field. But, rather than choosing just any details of their fieldwork to portray, they select those that signify the theorized storyline that shortly will be developed. Bringing in the field piques readers' expectation that "real" and interesting organizational situations will be portrayed; it also provides them an orienting glimpse into the storyline that will be developed. In this respect, the beginning affords an important opportunity to depict "memorable examples of . . . issues and concepts" (Gephart, 2004) being investigated in the broader disciplinary community, and that signify our storylines.

In the first example (Barker, 1993), we are presented with Ronald's ironic account of being more closely observed at work now that the small manufacturing company has restructured into self-managing teams. The article begins with a quote from Ronald that is interpreted by the author.

> I don't have to sit there and look for the boss to be around, and if the boss is not around, I can sit there and talk to my neighbor or do what I want. Now the whole team is around me and the whole team is observing what I'm doing.
>
>   "Ronald," a technical worker in a small manufacturing company, gave me this account one day while I was observing his work team. Ronald works in what contemporary writers call a postmodern organization which is not structured as a rule-based hierarchy. He works with a team of peers who are

all equally responsible for managing their own work behaviors. But Ronald described an unexpected consequence of this team-based design. With his voice concealed by work noise, Ronald told me that he felt more closely watched now than when he worked under the company's old bureaucratic system. He said that while his old supervisor might tolerate someone coming in a few minutes late, for example, his team had adopted a "no tolerance" policy on tardiness and that members monitored their own behaviors carefully. (p. 408)

The introductory paragraphs of our second example, a study of risk and blame in disaster sensemaking (Gephart, 1993, pp. 1465–1466), vividly portray the context of the study—a gas-line explosion, and the allocation of blame subsequent to the explosion—and also point toward the developing storyline of organizational sensemaking about risk management.

Gas Blast Blamed on Wind Shift

A sudden shift in the wind may have triggered a spectacular pipeline explosion that critically injured five Big City men Tuesday night. The gas in the high-pressure 51-cm pipeline was probably ignited by equipment brought in to repair a leak, says [the] director of operations for the Western Pipe Lines. (Newspaper article, February 20, 1985)

Foreman Was a Family Man

[Western] Pipe Lines (ltd.) lost a 30 year employee when Merv Ginter died in the burn unit of University Hospital Monday. But to the members of his family, Ginter's death represents the loss of a husband, a father and a grandfather. (Newspaper article, March 5, 1985)

Pipeline Worker Dies

[A second] of five pipeline workers injured in an explosion died Wednesday. (Newspaper article, March 7, 1985)

Public Inquiry Testimony

In light of the serious nature and tragic consequences of the leak, the Board is holding this public inquiry into the accident. The purpose of this inquiry, therefore, is to permit the Board to determine whether any changes should be made in the way that [Western Pipe Lines] operates, or the way in which [it] is regulated by the Board, in order to prevent similar accidents in the future;

it is not the primary purpose of this inquiry to fix any blame for what happened. (Chairperson of government energy board, March 26, 1985)

At other times, authors take us to the field by telling rather than showing us that something significant happened. In each of the following two examples, the authors do this by taking us to the scene of action. The first example (Maitlis, 2004, pp. 1275–1276) takes us to a meeting of board directors who must decide the principal conductor's future with the orchestra, an event that points toward the developing storyline of how a CEO influences (and fails to influence) board decision making.

The directors of a major British symphony orchestra were meeting to make a critical decision about the orchestra's principal conductor. His contract was due to expire in two months' time, and a decision had to be made whether to renew it for a further three-year term or look for a new individual to fill this key role. At the start of the board meeting, the orchestra's chief executive officer (CEO) highlighted several areas of dissatisfaction with the conductor, including the musician's fear of him, the lukewarm reception he had received from audiences, and his failure to bring recording contracts to the orchestra. The CEO concluded his presentation with a recommendation to the board not to renew the principal conductor's contract. There then followed a heated discussion among several board members. . . . After one and a half hours of frequently circular debate, the chairman of the board became impatient and closed the discussion, instructing the CEO to meet with the principal conductor and offer a contract renewal. The board had rejected the CEO's recommendation.

In the next example, Wilson Ng and Christian De Cock (2002) take us to the scene of a hostile takeover, which they describe as a "watershed in Singapore corporate history" that provides an entrée into examining how the role of discursive performances shaped the emerging battle.

Valentine's Day 1995 was a watershed in Singapore corporate history. On this day, Antony, one of Singapore's oldest companies, launched a hostile takeover bid for Cleo, a "home-grown success story" which was one of Singapore's best known companies. The hostility of Antony's bid surprised the local market; analysts could not recall the last hostile takeover. The brazenness of Antony's pursuit caught public attention . . .

To gain public support, Antony executed a meticulous public relations programme which centred on the appointment of a new chairman for Cleo. Antony's board of directors nominated a local Chinese entrepreneur with great public stature for this role . . . [and who] expected [their nominee as

Chairman] to cement control of Cleo on Antony's behalf. . . . Initially the new chairman seemed to reward the faith invested in him as he began an "extensive program to review and restructure [Cleo's] operations" . . . but appearances deceived. Behind a façade of corporate unity, Cleo's new chairman initiated a power struggle to seize control of Cleo. He eventually took exclusive, personal control of Cleo and left Antony, the majority shareholder, without an effective voice in running Cleo.

The public were never aware of any "battle in the boardroom." Instead, public statements painted an official story of change as well organized and professionally managed with a successful outcome never in doubt. However, beneath this level of public perception several other storylines gave conflicting accounts of how Cleo's restructuring was progressing. These various storylines form the crux of our investigation as they point to the importance of discursive performances given by key protagonists in carving out positions of power. (pp. 23–24)

NOVEL USE OF METHODOLOGY SECTIONS

Some authors have rearranged space allocated for methodology sections by not only depicting data collection and analyses, but also portraying the field itself in a manner that enhances their developing storyline. In creating methodology sections, these authors are changing the name to broader terms or are inserting sections dedicated to describing the fieldwork context, such as "research setting," "research site" or "field site." Note how each of the following examples uses this rearranged space to describe particular settings and events that link the fieldwork to the core ideas of the storyline being developed.

Our first example, an article on organizing moves in software support hot-lines by Brian Pentland (1992), argues that knowledge is situated performance and that practice theory can provide the conceptual foundation for this view. Subdividing the "Method" section into Research Setting, Access and Observation, and Data, he develops the storyline by using the research setting to establish a hot line in a software organization as the appropriate setting to study routine and gain theoretically relevant insights into knowledge as situated performance. His discussion of research setting begins with,

A hot line is a convenient setting in which to study service performances because the work consists of large numbers of discrete units . . . that are processed fairly routinely. Lave (1988) argued that everyday, routine activities of this kind are especially appropriate topics for practice theory. (pp. 533–534)

In subdividing a general "Research Focus" section, the second example (Reay, Golden-Biddle, & GermAnn, 2006) creates a subsection, "Nurse Practitioners in Alberta." Here, the authors describe the general governance structure of health care in Canada and detail the Nurse Practitioner role in terms of typical services, recent growth in numbers and places of work. This information not only situates nurse practitioners in a particular geographical context that may be different for some readers, but also in depicting the historical developments and present work situations, contextualizes its developing storyline.

The final example, by Beth Bechky (2003), differentiates the "Methods" and "Analysis" sections, subdividing methods into Research Site and Data Sources. The first two paragraphs of "Research Site" provide detail about the site, "EquipCo," that explicitly develops its suitability for investigating cross-occupational knowledge sharing. She explains,

> EquipCo was an ideal site to study the dynamics of cross-occupational knowledge sharing. As a high-tech manufacturing firm that designed its own products, EquipCo had a strong formal organization, characterized by the importance of the distribution of engineering drawings. Additionally, EquipCo faced a quickly changing market, and therefore new prototypes were being built all the time. The many occupational communities involved in the production process needed to effectively share their knowledge to get these machines out the door. In a manufacturing organization, much of the feedback about the production process occurs during product "handoffs," when responsibility for the product shifts from engineering to prototyping to manufacturing. These handoffs provided many opportunities to witness the ways in which the informal social and work organization made the transformation of local understandings possible. (p. 315)

DATA–THEORY COUPLING

In representing our fieldwork through data excerpts, we have the opportunity to bring together the worlds of the field and academy. We are looking in two directions: toward the research situation to the forms and processes of organizational life encountered in the field, and toward the academy to the literature and processes of creating research space for the study encountered in our writing. Underscoring this relationship between depicting data and conveying their theorized significance, the literary critic Wayne Booth (1961) distinguishes between "showing" and "telling." He explains that the "accumulation of accurately observed detail cannot satisfy us for long; only if the details are made to tell, only if they are weighted with a significance" do they hold our attention (p. 114). We show data and tell their significance. We theorize the fragments of life we show. Consequently, primarily in the middle sections of our manuscripts, we couple the fragments of organizational life with our theorizing as we develop storylines. The life we portray is always theorized as, reciprocally, the theory we develop is always contextualized. Here, we explore a few examples that illustrate how authors variously relate the showing and telling of data in developing storylines.

Telling, Showing, and Telling

Some authors use a sandwich structure to couple their data with theory: they first explain the core idea that will be depicted in the following data, then show that data, and finally tell more abstractly what the data showed. In the first example (Kahn, 1993, pp. 548–549), we are told and then shown the nature of caregiving that flows between a social worker and her client in a social service agency.

> Other aspects of the flow pattern are highlighted in the following excerpt of a phone conversation between a social worker and her client, a mother of four boys. The care that the social worker gave her client was a rich concentration of each of the dimensions of caregiving. She made a lot of time available to the woman, patiently inquired about and attended to her story, showed respect and empathy for her effort and struggles, supported her with information meant to empower her to take control of her life, and offered such care consistently during the conversation. Her end of the conversation included this passage:

> *I called to see how things are going. I'm glad you're able to use this phone at work. How are the matches going? (Listens) Good. I'm glad. How did you feel about that? (Listens) You sound like you handled that well. (Listens) I'll get back to you about the free shoes we have. I definitely have you in mind and will start to have a bit more time. Were you able to apply to some of the housing projects I sent you information about? (Listens) I'll keep my eye out and when I see things I'll send them to you. (Listens) You have to remember to do something for yourself. With four kids and another 100 at the day-care center during the day, you have to do for yourself. Get together with other people, adults at the Center. Make that a priority.*

This passage shows the social worker patiently listening and inquiring into her client's experience, making room for the woman to be present emotionally ("How did you feel about that?") and concretely ("Were you able to apply?").

This example begins by telling the dimensions of caregiving that flow between social workers and their clients as situated in the *phone conversation between a social worker and her client, a mother of four boys.* The author follows this telling with showing by materializing those dimensions in the depiction of the actual phone conversation. He returns at the conclusion of the excerpt to telling again, in his more general translation of the caregiver's behavior. The distinction between telling and showing is further highlighted by the manuscript's switching into a different font as the author changes from narrating the theory in the voice of the observer and organizational scholar to demonstrating it in the voice of an organizational actor, and back again.

A second example, from an article by Connie Gersick (1988), proposes a midpoint transition as a critical development event in work teams.

The Midpoint Transition

As each group approached the midpoint between the time it started work and its deadline, it underwent great change. The following excerpts from transitional meetings illustrate the nature and depth of this change. Particular points to notice are members' comments about time and their behavior toward external supervisors.

Excerpt 5(E5) The students begin their meeting on the sixth day of an 11-day span.

1. Rajeev: I think, what he said today in class—I have, already, lots of criticism on our outline. What we've done now is ok, but we need a lot more emphasis on organization design than what we—I've been doing up till now.

2. Jack: I think you're right. We've already been talking about [X]. We should be talking more about [Y].

3. Rajeev: We've done it—and it's super—but we need to do other things, too.

4. (Bert agrees.)

5. Jack: After hearing today's discussion— we need to say [X] more directly. And we want to say more explicitly that.

6. Rajeev: Should we be organized and look at the outline? We should know where we're going.

(The group goes quickly through the outline members had prepared for the meeting, noting changes and additions they want to make.)

7. Rajeev: The problem is we're very short on time. (p. 23)

It is significant that Rajeev's remark, "We're very short on time," was only the second comment about the adequacy of the time the group had for the project, and it marked a switch from Jack's early sentiment that "we've got some more time" (E2,6). A new sense of urgency marked this meeting.

As was also the case in the example of caregiving by a social worker, Connie Gersick begins by making a theoretical point: The development of work teams is characterized by a midpoint transition. Then, before proceeding to show the enactment of midpoint in a particular work team, she directs readers to "notice" the elements of that transition, time and change (in their behavior toward authority) in the fragment of team life that she then presents. Finally, having shown the data of team life, she once again calls readers' attention to the element of time, and in so doing, underscores and advances the theoretical framework.

Minimal Telling, Showing, Telling, More General Telling

Authors also develop theorized storylines by immediately showing data (usually after a subheading that minimally signals theory), then telling the theoretical significance of those data after they have been shown. These showing–telling episodes then build into a more general discussion of theory (telling) that is demarcated from the last section of the article, for example, the discussion or conclusion.

Our first example of this form of coupling data and theory is the article by Jane Dutton and Janet Dukerich (1991) examining how individuals and organizations make sense of and enact "nontraditional and emotional strategic issues," using the particular issue of homelessness. A dominant portion of their empirical portrait, then, concerns showing how the issue of homelessness changes in interpretation over time. The section, "Interpretations of and Actions on Homelessness," depicts five chronological phases, distinguished by key events, major interpretations and major actions regarding the homelessness issue. The data are both discussed in the text and summarized in a figure depicting the history of the homelessness issue. In the next section, "The Role of Organizational Identity and Image," the authors develop the more general telling component of the storyline, linking it to relevant literature.

Our second example is the article by James Barker (1993, pp. 419–433), which examines the evolution of concertive control in self-managing teams from value consensus to normative rules. The major portion of representing his field work is the middle section, titled "The Development of Concertive Control" and subdivided into sections denoting the three phases of development: "Consolidation and Value Consensus," "Emergence of Normative Rules," and "Stabilization and Formalization of the Rules." These titles represent minimal telling as they arrange and link data representation with the theorized story-line. Then, within each phase, James Barker uses both employees' words and his own to depict the emergent dynamics:

> Phase I began with the chaos of Jack's abrupt changing of the manufacturing area to teams over that weekend in August 1988. While the workers knew that the change was coming, they still walked into a whole new experience on Monday morning. Bonnie, an original ISE employee, described the scene for me:
>
> > Well it was mass confusion. Nobody knew where they were sitting, what team they were on. They had an idea of what was going on at that point and what the team aspect was all about. As far as details, no idea! So, basically, everybody was just kind of like WOW, this is kinda fun! (p. 419)

Thus, he details concrete events constituting this phase, for example, "Jack assigned workers to the three new teams by drawing names out of a hat" and makes comments still quite close to the events, such as, "The challenge for the teams during this phase was learning how to work together and supervise themselves functionally." Then, as the description of the phase draws to a close, James Barker (1993) engages in more general telling, as represented in the following comments:

> This vignette depicts how the team concertively reached a value consensus that, in turn, controlled individual and collective work . . .
>
> Although there were slight differences, this value consensus and these decision premises emerged powerfully and with remarkable consistency across the new teams . . .
>
> There were four key points in the consolidation phase . . . (pp. 422–424)

Our final example is Bob Gephart's (1993) study of disaster sensemaking. In a section titled, "Analysis," this article shows the data: individual stories of the disaster by the assistant district manager, the worker, the district manager and the board. These stories are conveyed more thoroughly in the accompanying tables. The stories are developed in the text, primarily by showing verbatim, transcribed data, though some "telling" enters near the end of each story in reflective comments about the data made by the author. However, the "telling" explicitly begins with the subsection of "Key Words" in which conceptually related clusters, for instance, rules and policies, and safety, are developed from a textual analysis of the transcript data. Finally, the more general telling is found in a separate section following Analysis, titled, "Summary of Findings."

STORYLINES WITH FIELD AND THEORY COMPLICATIONS

The final innovation involves the representation of both field and theory-based complications in our storylines. Since disciplinary journals require theoretical complications, for example, gaps or lacuna, the vast majority of articles published in them construct such complications as part of their storylines. However, some articles also articulate a field-based complication alongside, and cohering with the theoretical complication. In so doing, these articles create the opportunity to resonate more deeply with readers because they portray theoretical significance as well as "real-life" significance: that is, real people confronted with significant problems, who in their efforts to deal with the problems, are fundamentally changed (Franklin, 1994).

In this section, we profile one exemplar article, "The Organizational and Interorganizational Development of Disasters," by Barry Turner (1976). Let's examine in greater detail what it could look like to write theoretical and field significance into our work. In the following excerpt, he constructs a field-based complication, which we italicize (pp. 378–379).

> Administrative organizations may be thought of as cultural mechanisms developed to set collective goals . . . Given this concern with future objectives, analysts have paid considerable attention to the manner in which organizational structures are patterned to cope with unknown events—or uncertainty—in the future facing the organization and its environment (Crozier, 1964; Thompson, 1967; Lawrence and Lorsch, 1967).
>
> Uncertainty creates problems for action. Actors' organizations resolve these problems by following rules of thumb, using rituals, relying on habitual patterns, or, more self-consciously, by setting goals and making plans to reach them . . . But since organizations are indeterminate open systems, particularly in their orientation to future events (Thompson, 1967:10), members of organizations can never be sure that their present actions will be adequate for the attainment of their desired goals.
>
> Prediction is made more difficult by the complex and extensive nature of the tasks . . . When a task which was formerly small enough to be handled

amenably grows to an unmanageable size, resources may be increased to handle the larger problem . . . (Hirsch, 1975) . . . Alternatively, the task to be handled may shrink to fit the resources available or the amount of information . . . (Meier, 1965) . . . The success of these strategies, however, turns on the issue of whether the simplified diagnosis of the present and likely future situation is accurate enough to enable the organizational goals to be achieved without encountering unexpected difficulties that lead on to catastrophe.

The central difficulty, therefore, lies in discovering which aspects of the current set of problems facing an organization are prudent to ignore and which should be attended to, and how an acceptable level of safety can be established in carrying out this exercise.

This complication is grounded in the field; it consists of a real-life problem that members of a variety of organizations find significant. Which problems should be attended to so that we can avoid catastrophe? This complication matters, and in its articulation, places the field context central and figural to the article. To bring home the theoretical significance of this issue, Barry Turner incorporates relevant literature on uncertainty into his discussion. Note, however, that rather than problematizing that literature, he uses it to contextualize the field complication. In this respect, he stories the theory.

He then proceeds to construct the theoretical complication, which is derived from the field complication, and which we italicize in the excerpt below.

Wilensky (1967) has suggested that to deal with such situations, one must discover how to recognize high-quality intelligence about the problem at hand, using the term intelligence in its military sense. Wilensky's criteria for high-quality intelligence are that it should be "clear, timely, reliable, valid, adequate and wide-ranging." . . . *This is excellent as a normative statement of what is desirable, but it does little in practical situations to offer tests of clarity, timeliness, or adequacy of intelligence. One means which Wilensky did put forward for tackling these latter issues, however, is by the examination of failures of intelligence, these being more important than failures of control. Taking up this suggestion, this article considers the manner in which such an approach could be used to begin to identify, as Wilensky (1967:121) puts it, "the conditions that foster the failure of foresight . . ."* (Turner, 1976, p. 379)

This time, the complication is grounded in the extant literature, and in particular, in the work of Wilensky. However, the theoretical complication does not leave the field behind. This time it is used as a context of relevance for the theory, grounded in how it helps "practical situations." Thus, the storyline embodies two central, figural complications—one based in the field and the other in the literature—and implies that resolutions will be developed for both. These complications are so integrally interwoven that it is difficult to discern where one begins and the other ends.

Finally, Turner (1976) develops an added twist by complicating the complications, and in so doing, renders them more significant for members of both the field and academic worlds. He first defines the type of disasters that he will examine as those that "present problems of explanation," and then continues:

> The concern, here, therefore, is to make an examination of some large-scale disasters that are potentially foreseeable and potentially avoidable, and that, at the same time, are sufficiently unexpected and sufficiently disruptive to provoke a cultural reassessment of the artefacts and precautions available to prevent such occurrences. The intention of this examination is to look for a set of patterns that precede such disasters. Having identified such a pattern, one can go on to ask whether it can also be found in the preconditions for other major organizational failures which do not necessarily lead to loss of life, but which, nevertheless, provoke the disruption of cultural assumptions about the efficacy of current precautions, such as the collapse of a public company . . . (p. 380)

We want to continue reading in order to gain insight into how to prevent disasters and organizational failures. Does he develop patterns, and if so, what are they? For it is this insight into disasters, if disclosed, that resolves the significant complications. By constructing a storyline that integrates cohering field and theoretical complications, Barry Turner opens up his work and ideas to readers in both worlds.

In this chapter, we have explored some representational choices authors face when drawing on fieldwork to develop theorized storylines. As authors, we have available to us our vast field data, often reaching hundreds and even thousands of pages. Which of the hundreds of collected experiences and stories do we select to write into our texts? How do we incorporate our field engagement to develop—vitalize and enrich—our theorized storylines? Edmonson (1984) points to the need for selectivity in the choice of what from organizational life is to be included in our write-ups. These "condensed examples" should not only illustrate theoretical insights, but also embody vividness that brings the points alive in a way that evokes the human interest of readers. The examples should draw readers into the organizational situations studied and invest them in the storylines developed. We have shown how authors variously seek to accomplish this in their texts through the construction of compelling beginnings, the novel use of methodology sections, specified and coherent data–theory coupling, and the creation of twin sets of complications based in the field and academy. Examples such as those highlighted throughout this chapter develop the theorized storyline by providing vivid and significant examinations of organizational life that connect with us as readers.

FOUR

CHARACTERIZING THE STORYTELLER

L et's begin by taking a brief excursion to ancient Greece—to one of the Platonic dialogues. Here, we find Socrates about to deliver a speech that challenges the arguments posed by a young man, Phaedrus, in an address just delivered on the subject of love. Socrates is in somewhat of an awkward position. He finds the arguments he must make in his speech to be morally offensive. Consequently, in anticipation of the words to follow, he declares, "I shall cover my head before I begin; then I can rush through my speech at top speed without looking at you and breaking down for shame" (Hamilton & Cairns, 1961, p. 237). Although Socrates is delivering an oral speech as opposed to offering a written text, the image of him covering his head and dashing through his presentation in a vain attempt to conceal himself from the words he is speaking allegorically points to two significant dimensions of characterizing the storyteller in our work; how authors portray themselves in their work, and whether or not audiences regard this portrait of the author as consistent with their expectations.

Socrates' actions first direct our attention to the author's character as a central aspect of any discourse, whether it is spoken or written. The text Socrates is about to deliver is one from which he would prefer to dissociate himself; however, the image of the shrouded speaker only highlights the relationship between Socrates and, in this case, his spoken words. Similarly, in the act of racing through the words, almost as if trying to escape them as they fall from his lips, Socrates actually reaffirms the connection between author and text. Second, Socrates references the audience, "you," to whom he directs his speech. In both oral and written discourse, an audience is established. The obvious difference is that in written discourse that audience is implied; authors neither see the readers nor engage them in face-to-face interaction. Nevertheless, a particular audience is imagined, and authors in part shape their character in the text according to what they think this implied audience views as acceptable and trustworthy. What we are asserting, then, is that authorial character is always constructed by the author in the text, even in our "scientific" journal articles. To build on Socrates' example and paraphrase the literary critic, Booth (1961), authors can never choose to vanish completely from their texts; they can only pick the disguise in which they will appear.

The preceding discussion of Socrates, implied authorial character, and implied readers takes us to the thesis of this chapter: that, in various ways, intentionally or unintentionally, we express a character in our written accounts. This does not mean, however, that only one type of character is crafted. As we will see, although the institutional scientist is the dominant character crafted in journal articles, the degree and intensity of this character varies. Increasingly over the past decade, within general institutional delimitations, more personal and human authorial depictions are being composed in journal articles.

To briefly highlight the distinction between a more institutional and a more human and individual expression of authorial character, consider how the social scientist is represented in the following two excerpts from the same article. The paper's purpose is to rebut a challenge to a particular form of narrative research—one that focuses on stories of personal illness and suffering:

> Reacting to the charge that personal narratives, especially illness narratives, constitute a "blind alley" that misconstrues the essential nature of narrative by substituting a therapeutic for a sociological view of the person, this article speaks back to critics who regard narratives of suffering as privileged, romantic, and/or hyperauthentic. The author argues that this critique of personal narrative rests on an idealized and discredited theory of inquiry. . . . (from Bochner, 2001, p. 131)

The institutional depiction of the scientist is evident in the use of a familiar "professional" academic writing style and in the portrayal of the author as disengaged and dispassionate, achieved textually by having "the article" speak back and the arguing author refer to himself in the third person. Later in the paper, the expressed authorial character changes as the dispassionate scientific representation gives way to an engaged passionate human perspective:

As I'm writing this critical response to these articles, a whole slew of thoughts and feelings run through me . . . I don't find their evidence, their reasoning, their citations, or their illustrations at all convincing, and I know I can point to evidence, arguments, authorities, and cases that will unravel the loose threads they've woven. I've done a lot of this writing over the years . . . On the other hand, there's this personal voice that's also trying to get out of me, and I'm having difficulty containing it . . . Something very deep inside me erupted, something that's accumulated during 30 years of teaching and research. Jane Tompkins (1987) calls this feeling "old anger . . ." (from Bochner, 2001, pp. 133–134)

In this chapter, then, we are concerned with how as storytellers we express our authorial character in journal articles. We begin with a general introduction to the ways in which we textually depict ourselves as institutional and human scientists. Then, we consider three key areas in which we craft our character as storytellers. These are: depicting the relationship between ourselves and the situations and people we study; indicating our technical competence as researchers; and, unique to qualitative researchers who collect data close up *in* organizations, conveying keen and detailed field knowledge in our access to and construction of the field story. Our discussion recognizes that we have some choices about the authorial character we compose in our writing; in so doing, it raises the question of who we want to be as storytellers in the articles we write—what kind of self as institutional and human scientists we will craft in our work.

STORYTELLER IN THE GUISE OF INSTITUTIONAL AND HUMAN SCIENTIST

When seeking to publish in our disciplinary journals, we need to appear in guises that establish recognizable characters that are regarded as credible by our readers. In these journals, the implied readers are reviewers and editors, as well as other colleagues in the discipline. These readers have been trained in the conduct and philosophy of science through extended professional schooling and, often, have conducted work in a similar area. Thus, they come to the reading of our manuscripts with particular points of view regarding the topic, and with internalized norms for conducting, reading, and writing science. Geertz (1988) forcefully makes the point about this relationship between authorial character and reader receptivity, insisting that authors' abilities to establish themselves as part of their readers' particular disciplinary community is basic to getting their manuscripts published, read, and cited.

The issue of depicting a character receptive to social science readers perhaps more specifically faces researchers who rely on qualitative data. As Glaser and Strauss (1967), Strauss (1987), and Strauss and Corbin (1990) point out, qualitative work will be read, and often evaluated, by those who use quantitatively based research methodology. These readers bring with them expectations that the articles they read will express a traditional scientific character.

This situation is rapidly changing, however, for at least two reasons. First, a re-evaluation of the role of the researcher within scientific research is among the effects of social science's "interpretive" turn toward the humanities (Bruner, 1996; Geertz, 1983, 1988; Rabinow & Sullivan, 1987) and its understanding of the social world not as an exterior object but as a subjectively lived construct. Specifically, the interpretive perspective has led to an emphasis on the reflexive nature of the research process and the subjectivity inherent in constructions of meaning made by both research subjects and researchers (Mottier, 2005). The person of the researcher is seen as firmly embedded in any inquiry effort. Second, greater numbers of qualitative researchers are now ad hoc reviewers, editorial board members, and editors. This points to a situation in flux where authors develop the character of institutional scientist in their work but also, increasingly, they may portray more of this scientist's human character. Furthermore, in so doing they demonstrate some flexibility in their adherence to more traditional institutional canons for scientific texts. Consequently, there is growing variation in how the scientist is depicted.

Consistent with the use of a "scientistic style" in academic writing, as documented by McCloskey (1994), qualitative work does portray the storyteller as a "scientific" character, and thereby inserts the mark of the institution. We would not expect otherwise. Accordingly, we portray ourselves as members in good standing of the professional community by demonstrating our facility with the Academy's writing conventions. Some of these include: following norms for organizing our research articles as expected into introductory literature reviews, methods, findings, and discussions; representing information and ideas though the use of tables and figures; engaging in the practice of referencing; and using our particular vernacular, such as "drawing on research on . . . ," "this paper argues . . . ," "a limitation of this research is . . . ," "we develop a model of . . . ," and so on. Furthermore, through use of language codes associated with qualitative research, for example, "in-depth interviews," "rich insights," "participant observation," "inductive research," "respondent validation," and the like, we mark ourselves as members of that community within the broader Academy.

At the same time as we portray our institutional character through our facility with the organizational, representational, and language conventions of the research article, we also make choices about how we, as the agents of the research, will or will not appear in the texts we write. Most often, as Van Maanen (1988) indicates, the form of authorial [non]-presence is expressed in the articles we write. We choose to remain out of view. This is consistent with an institutional depiction of research being conducted without any suggestion of the personal subjectivity of the researchers. Eliminating the human scientist from the text is compatible with an assumption that the removal of possible researcher biases is both desirable and possible. The examples below, which draw on the passive voice, are typical of this authorial characterization. Can you see the authors?

> This paper reports on research that tells the story of nurse managers' attempts to provide a 24 hour service. Although research was contextualized within five National Health Service general hospital trusts in the United Kingdom, the outcomes are not merely *about* the NHS. It is argued that ward and directorate general management (referred to as middle managers), possessing delegated responsibility, are considered to be empowered. Such empowerment is accompanied by widely experienced anxiety. As in any exchange, anxiety is the price of empowerment. An escalatory and contagious process is observed which exaggerates "normal" stress and challenge among middle managers into a state of self-perceived angst. . . . This paper draws on data to demonstrate the delegation process. (from Brooks, 2003, pp. 125–126)

> This research considers whether interpretive techniques can be used to enhance our understanding of computer-mediated discussions. The case study considered in this research is the use of a group support system (GSS) to support employee discussions about gender equity in a university. Transcripts of the four discussions were analyzed using two analysis techniques: a positivist approach, which was focused on the GSS sessions themselves, and an interpretive approach which broadened the scope to include contextual considerations as well. What emerged from the positivist analysis was the conclusion of effective group behavior directed toward consensus around alternative solution scenarios. What emerged from the interpretive analysis was evidence of multiple, rich types of information at three levels: cognitive, affective, and behavioral. The interpretive analysis also uncovered the absence of shared consciousness about the issue and imbalanced participation in the sessions. (from Trauth & Jessup, 2000, p. 43)

> This exploratory, descriptive study examined the search and selection process for an aged care facility following discharge of a family member from an

acute setting. Few studies have examined this process and its effects on families. Individuals from 25 families where a family member had been recently admitted to an aged care facility following discharge from an acute setting were interviewed. This article reports participants' perceptions of the search and selection process and its effect on the family. Five major themes emerged from the data: good fortune, wear and tear on the sponsor, dealing with the system, urgency, and adjusting. (from Cheek & Ballantyne, 2001, p. 221)

Through this characterization, we portray the processes and nonhuman elements such as the "research," "analysis," and "papers" or "studies" (rather than people) as advancing the research enterprise.

A slightly more visible representation of the author, yet still consistent with institutional expectation, is achieved through use of the third person. In this case, the institutional characterization is achieved by representing researchers through their institutional roles, for example as "authors" and "researchers." This is evident in the following example:

In this article, the authors address the boundaries of institutional structures, the dynamics of their configuration, and the nature of their permeability. The authors explored these issues in Israel, where the changing relationship of bio- and alternative medicine elucidates recent processes of professional boundary redefinition. They used qualitative methods to analyze in-depth interviews in clinics and hospitals where alternative and biomedical practitioners work under the formal auspices of publicly sponsored biomedical organizations. (from Shuval & Mizrachi, 2004, pp. 675–690)

While such representations consistent with an institutional portrayal prevail in our research writing, authors also choose to make themselves visible by appearing in the first person in their writing. Writing themselves into the text at the same time as they draw on other institutional writing conventions, these authors portray a scientific character whose human face is more visible.

In this study, we explore seven in-depth cases of high-technology acquisitions and develop an empirically grounded model of technology and capability transfer during acquisition implementation. We assess how the nature of the acquired firms' knowledge based resources, as well as multiple dimensions of acquisition implementation, have both independent and interactive effects on the successful appropriation of technologies and capabilities by the acquirer. Our inquiry contributes to the growing body of research examining the transfer of knowledge both between and within organizations. (from Ranft & Lord, 2002, p. 420)

In the above example, Annette Ranft and Michael Lord portray a human character through use of the first person pronoun. In this way, researchers reveal themselves as they "*explore*" and "*assess.*" At the same time, their institutional character is implicated as they describe their exploring and assessing activities in scientific vernacular; for instance, "*independent and interactive effects*" as well the phrase "*contributes to the growing body of research.*" In the following example, Paaige Turner renders visible the human scientist through the use of first person, while also marking the profession in her use of a familiar roadmap to organize her article.

In this article, I provide a case study of the intersection of traditional and alternative health care practices. . . . It is only once we understand the experiences of those who live at this intersection that we will be able to make informed decisions about how to bring alternative medicine into the mainstream. Accordingly, I first provide an overview of the current growth in alternative medicine and birth practices; second, I define a postmodern conceptualization of paradox; finally, I articulate the experiences of one group of birth care providers, who operate a free-standing birth center, as they attempt to live at the intersection of their own beliefs and traditional constructions of birth and birth practices. Specifically, I see these experiences as embedded within a web of meaning that alternative birth care providers experience as simultaneously marginalizing part of their occupational identity while allowing them to operate within the dominant sociopolitical system. (from Turner, 2004, pp. 644–645)

In the final two examples, the authors more strongly reveal themselves as human agents in the inquiry process, revealing an analytic self-consciousness and more of their individual human face (at the same time as their depictions of themselves' going about the work of research simultaneously portray their institutional character). In the illustration that follows, Ulrike Schultz reveals her gender, age, and marital status by elaborating how it shaped her data gathering efforts.

Being a woman meant that I established an easier rapport and a closer relationship with the women in the field than I did with the men. Among the three librarians, all of whom were women, and the three system administrators, one of whom was a woman, I was more quickly accepted as an insider than I was by the four competitive intelligence analysts, all of whom were men. I was particularly aware of gender roles when it came to contact outside the work setting. For instance, as a single, 30 year old woman, I could uninhibitedly ask other women to go to lunch; however, asking the men, most of whom were also older than me, was not as comfortable and seemed to require more of a justification. (from Schultze, 2000, p. 10)

In the next excerpt, Barbara Czarniawska discusses the activities of research in more human terms as she builds an argument that organizational culture as conceptualized in American scholarship offers little for the understanding of organizations in socialist economies. In particular, she narrates her personal efforts to apply the concept. She is *"both a student and a member"* of Polish organizations, and as a researcher she *"tried to relate"* the concept as it appeared in American thinking to her Polish context but *"had serious problems"* doing so. While a strong human depiction of the researcher is offered, her mastery and application of her topic and use of the referencing convention simultaneously points to her membership in the Academy.

> When I first encountered the concept of organizational culture in American organizational thinking, I tried to relate the notion to the Polish organizational reality of which I was both a student and a member. I assumed, taking from the numerous definitions what seemed the least ambiguous, that an organizational culture is a shared set of values (what should be done and why), beliefs (how things are should be done), and material and non-material artifacts (Sathe, 1983; Schein, 1983a). Such a set shows an internal consistency, i.e. is perceived as a system by the members of the organization, or at least a significant part of them, and differentiates an organization from other organizations. However, I had serious problems in finding organizational cultures in the Polish organizations I knew. There were very distinct traces of "occupational cultures" (Van Maanen & Barley, 1984) but these extended beyond organizations. (from Czarniawska, 1986, pp. 313–314)

INSTITUTIONAL AND HUMAN STORYTELLER IN RELATIONSHIP TO THE STUDIED

Representing the style of no style, or "windowpane prose" discussed in Chapter 1, the institutional scientist is implied in the crafting of an objective and impersonal relationship between researcher and research situation. The institutional scientist is implicated in a recounting of the field story as it really happened (McCloskey, 1990, 1994; Van Maanen, 1988), as if it were a straightforward rendering of the facts, with minimal, personal involvement. An objective and impersonal relationality is expressed when the people and situations studied from which the field story is crafted are presented as "data" to whom the researcher relates as sources of information and evidence. A more human relationality, on the other hand, is indicated by representations of the researcher engaging the studied in recognizably human terms.

A major way that we establish an objective relationality to the events, situations, and people studied, and thereby convey the character of the institutional scientist in our writing, is by presenting "data" to support and make evident our theorized storylines. As supporting evidence, the data acquire the ontological status of "factual statements" (McCloskey, 1994); they are presented as if they originated from a source other than the author, and represent opinions of persons other than the author. For example, we rarely use personal pronouns in the data sections, presenting the data as if independently collected. Moreover, we employ data as evidence to support, substantiate, and advance our theoretical points.

When writing up qualitative research for journal articles, we construct data as "evidence" in various ways. As Chapter 3 suggests, the most common practice is probably for authors to format the data differently in the text so that they stand out more readily from the analyses. For example, they use quotation marks, indent, and single-space their data. In some journals, a smaller font size is used for the presentation of verbatim data. This practice represents what the researched said and did as evidential informational for the storyteller's interpretations and conclusions.

Second, some authors directly seek to underscore their objective relationship to the studied, and thereby contribute to a scientific characterization consistent with institutional expectations. In the examples below, the authors emphasize objectivity relative to researcher interpretations.

> The basic facts of the Shoreham case are objectively verifiable . . . the size of Shoreham's losses (see Table 1) and the set of events leading up to this disaster are not . . . in dispute. Finally, evidence on the independent variables . . . was assembled from multiple sources, many of whom were arms-length observers of the phenomenon. (from Ross & Staw, 1993, p. 708)

> Data were obtained by using a videocamera fixed on the wall. . . . Use of videotaped data for observational research has both strengths and weaknesses. Recording from a remote camera is relatively unobtrusive, so behaviors are minimally affected. (from Morse & Pooler, 2002, p. 242)

Finally, a few authors emphasize a relationship to the studied as objective data by engaging in the practice of explicitly assessing the evidential strength of their data. For example, they categorize the types of data provided to support their theorized storyline according to whether it is "strong" or "modest" evidence. In particular, some authors use the following notation in their work. I = strong evidence from interviews, i = modest evidence from interviews; O = strong observational evidence, o = modest observational evidence; and so on. When data are arrayed and categorized with such weighting, the result conveys that there is overwhelming and impressive evidence for the theorized storyline.

We would like to issue a caution, however, concerning the practice of weighting data. When weighted, qualitative data convey an objectivity and quantifiable preciseness that, we believe, are impossible and undesirable to obtain. In a discussion with Robert Sutton, an author who has used weighting, he noted that, although weighting helps him analyze data, he now regards its use in articles as depicting "false rigor" that perhaps is inserted to "make quantitative researchers happy." In essence, weights wrap qualitative data with quantitative trappings, and while they certainly allude to a researcher's scientific character, in so doing they not only signal to reviewers that the work should be judged on quantitative terms, but more important, obfuscate the more subtle meanings that could be disclosed in more completely arraying the data.

In addition to depicting our research encounter with the situations, events, and people studied in ways that highlight an objective relationality, portrayals incorporating human engagements with the researched are also evident. These textual depictions highlight the storyteller's human character, and are achieved in various ways. For example, authors may write into their texts information-rich encounters in terms that highlight the human relationship between researcher and researched. In the excerpt that follows, Geoff Walsham and Sundeep Sahay (1999), who examine the use of geographical information systems (GIS) to assist public administration in India, narrate a story about being lost that highlights a familiar humanity in cross-cultural encounters. It both points to the human engagement between researchers and researched and also informs the understanding and use of this technology in the Indian context, thereby depicting both institutional and human character:

> A second divergence between Indian conceptualizations and those of the West, which is of particular relevance to GIS technology, concerns the existence of a map-based culture. Typical Indians will rarely, if ever, use maps in their daily life. For example, on one of our field visits to a GIS scientific

institution, we spent over an hour in the heat of the middle of the day trying to find the location of the institution in the town we had arrived at by asking local people. None of the Indian scientists, or for that matter, the Indian author of this paper, had considered the production or use of a map for this purpose and when he was jokingly queried by the non-Indian author of this paper, he was firmly told that "we don't use maps for this purpose in India." (pp. 49–50)

In the second example that depicts human relationality in research encounters that is also information rich, Kathy Charmaz (1999) is investigating suffering in chronic illness.

The following story is from an interview of Christine Danforth, a 43-year-old receptionist whom I interviewed for 7 years. Christine has lupus erythematosus, Sjögren's syndrome, and chronic pain from old back injuries, and her physical condition had worsened since our last talk. She described the first of eight recent hospitalizations:

I got the sores that are in my mouth, got in my throat and closed my throat up, so I couldn't eat or drink. And then my potassium dropped down to 2.0. I was on the verge of cardiac arrest. . . . That time when I went in they gave me 72 bottles of pure potassium, burned all my veins out.

I asked, "What does that mean, that it burned your veins out?" She said,

It hurts really bad; it's just because it's so strong and they can't dilute it with anything. . . .

Imagine Christine walking slowly and determinedly up the short sidewalk to my house. See her bent knees and lowered head as she takes deliberate steps. Christine looks weary and sad, her face as burdened with care as her body is encumbered by pain and pounds. Always large, she is heavier than I have ever seen her, startlingly so. (pp. 362–363)

Presented in these terms, it is difficult to construe the author's relationship as that between social scientist and research subject.

INSTITUTIONAL AND HUMAN PORTRAYALS AS TECHNICALLY COMPETENT STORYTELLER

A further way in which we establish our character as members in good standing of the Academic institution is through portrayals of ourselves engaging in the processes and procedures of our research, highlighting our technical competency by telling how we have adhered to particular canonical procedures for the conduct and analysis of the research. In the past we may have asked, to which canons do we adhere in our written accounts—those positivist canons traditionally associated with quantitative or those associated with qualitative research? Today, however, both the question and the reading of qualitative research are considerably more complicated. The qualitative research community has become increasingly varied and differentiated, with researchers drawing on a broad range of paradigmatic orientations, for example, positivist, interpretive, and critical, as well as different research traditions, such as ethnography, phenomenology, ethnomethodology, narrative studies, discourse analysis, deconstruction, and so on (see Patton, 2002, for a useful overview). Consequently, authors depict their institutional character by emphasizing adherence to more general, formal methodological procedures that are recognizable to the broader institutional community.

These portrayals may include procedures that address concerns more typically associated with quantitative research. Consider in the following illustration the absence of the individual author in using procedures (and language) typical for quantitative approaches.

> For example, when a set of non-equivalent dependent variables is predicted and found to result from a particular treatment or process, an investigator can be relatively confident that such an effect has indeed occurred. Likewise, if a consequence is predicted and found to result from a particular array of non-equivalent independent variables, a strong inference can similarly be made. (from Ross & Staw, 1993, p. 705)

Or, these portrayals may include procedures that address concerns more typically associated with qualitative research. In the following example, the authors' scientific character is depicted through adherence to procedures for identifying and selecting major themes in the research (of course the extensive use of referencing further legitimizes the procedures as well as reinforces that this is a scientific character).

> Finally, after comparison, emerging clusters of themes were inductively developed (cf. Norman, Redfern, Tomalin & Oliver, 1992). This summative analysis drew on studies by Cheek (1997) and Ekman and Segesten (1995). Attention throughout was paid to looking for "rival or competing themes or explanations" (Patton, 1990, p. 462) to consider the weight of evidence and "best fit between data and analysis" (Patton, 1990, p. 462). Similarly, instances and patterns that did not "fit" within the themes agreed on were

considered within their original contexts. This formed part of what Patton (1990) terms "weighing alternatives" rather than producing a report or analysis "in which all the data lead in a single-minded fashion, in a rising crescendo, towards an overwhelming presentation of a single point of view" (p. 464). (from Cheek & Ballantyne, 2001, p. 225)

As we noted above, though, qualitative methods have become increasingly differentiated; accordingly, the procedural depictions of a technically competent research execution are quite varied. Below are three depictions from three different qualitative approaches. In the first, the researchers draw on an approach called "Revealed Causal Mapping" derived from Cognitive Science:

> The revealed causal maps are derived from the transcribed interviews in five steps. This procedure (Dreher et al. 1999) is detailed in Appendix A. In the first step, the causal statements are derived from the interviews, following the guidelines suggested by Axelrod. The two main considerations in this step are to identify the causal connectors and to establish the reliability of the identification procedure. Causal linkages are identified by finding causal statement in the transcribed interviews. (from Nelson, Nadkarni, Narayanan, & Ghods, 2000, p. 486)

In the second example, the "older" qualitative tradition of ethnography is indicated. Galit Ailon-Souday and Gideon Kunda (2003, p. 1078) demonstrate adherence to the canons and procedures associated with this qualitative approach in their portrayal of data gathering, spending *a year* studying a single organization through very intensive data gathering, including *130 in-depth and unstructured interviews* and *participant observation* of *approximately 60* organizational events in order to gain an understanding of their research phenomenon—globalization—as *"an everyday lived experience."*

A final example indicates a researcher executing the analytic procedures of deconstruction to illuminate gender discrimination. Specifically, a story told by a corporate president about how his company "supported" a woman who had her baby by Caesarean section is deconstructed (and reconstructed) from feminist standpoint. This woman was central to a new product launch.

> This part of the deconstruction explores what is not said, what is left out of the Caesarean story (for a more general description of this kind of deconstructive move, see Macherey 1978, p. 60). The Caesarean story begins with the phrase, "We have a young woman . . . ," rather than "A young woman

works for us." This phrase situates the text at the juncture between the public and private domains and offers a redefinition of the usual employment contract. (from Martin, 1990, p. 344)

The above three examples indicate the character of the researchers as members of particular qualitative communities by their highlighting the methodological procedures associated with the various traditions. Whether they will be read as indicating a research character in good standing with the social science institution depends, however, on the research perspective, experience, and theoretical and methodological vocabulary of the articles' readers. Indeed, in the case of our final example, given that deconstruction derives from traditions in the humanities and rests on epistemological premises that are quite different from those traditionally held by social scientists, readers who are not familiar with its philosophical perspective and analytic tradition may interpret the authorial character portrayed as not of "scientific" character.

As with the other writing practices we have highlighted in this chapter, more personal and human depictions of researchers' executing their projects also enter into our writing. In its most basic form, these depictions include the authors' use of the first person pronoun to demonstrate a human rather than technical agency in carrying out the research. Thus, in the following example, Amy Edmondson writes herself into her account of the procedure she followed in her study to understand the role of teams in organizational learning:

Procedure. In the first phase of the research, I studied the strategy team, consisting of the CEO, five senior vice presidents, and two subsidiary presidents because it worked to develop a new business strategy. I invested considerable time studying this top management team compared with the other 11 teams in the sample because of the opportunity for extensive and longitudinal data through which both reflection and change might be observed. Over a six-month period, I observed and tape recorded five full-day meetings and conducted individual interviews with six of the eight team members. This allowed observation of the team-learning process over time. (Edmondson, 2002. p. 131)

In the above account the author is written into the text and her scientific character is implicated in the familiar activities in which she is engaged. Thus, the "I" in the text is described as studying, observing, tape recording, conducting interviews, and so on—professionally expected activities.

A stronger and more vivid presentation of authors' human character is evident in portrayals atypical for a scientific character, for instance, when the storyteller is provided a body and feelings, and especially when that body and feelings are brought into, rather than shut out of, the analytic process. In the example that follows, the storyteller outlines the research approach she follows, describing how her emotional and physical responses to what she heard and observed informed her data gathering about the work lives of midwives.

> In this study, I employ an embodied, interpretive interactionist methodology to focus on "the point of view that confers meaning on problematic symbolic action" (Denzin, 2001, p. 32). Specifically, an interpretive interactionist approach looks at problematic interactions as moments that individuals define themselves and relations to each other. Yet, as a participative observer, this process was an embodied one for me. I would listen to their stories and want to ask them, "Why don't you shout down the doctors?" or "why didn't you stop the doctor from doing what you know is wrong?" Thus, the tension I felt became my guide for my analysis. My experience, similar to that of other theorists (Clair, 1996; Hooks, 1982), suggests that tension is not necessarily a problem to be solved, but rather a moment of discovery. (from Turner, 2004, p. 649)

The humanity of the researcher is similarly strongly drawn in the following confessional account (Van Maanen, 1988) of a storyteller disclosing the personal beliefs, hopes, and assumptions in play as she went about the work of making field notes.

> Even though I acknowledged to myself that no observation or description could be free of interpretation and a subjective point of view, it was nevertheless important to me to separate, to the best of my ability, my personal reflections, speculations, and situated interpretations from the events "as they happened." I believed that this would allow me, once I had completed my fieldwork, to reinterpret my notes with the benefit of hindsight, a more holistic understanding, and a specific theory. I thus endeavored to record incidents as objectively as possible. This meant that I carefully described events from the perspective of a distant observer, presenting them in their rich detail and including myself as a subject in the scene. I made my impressions, reactions and interpretations as explicit as possible, pretending that they would be used by someone who was unfamiliar with my field site. In this way, I hoped to present incidents independently of myself, i.e. my assumptions, knowledge, emotions and experiences. (from Schultze, 2000, p. 16)

Before moving on to consider how qualitative researchers portray themselves as field knowledgeable storytellers, we'd like to reflect briefly on the fairly extensive referencing that accompanied authors' depictions of themselves at their work. Referencing, of course, is a hallmark of academic writing. When authors cite exemplary works, they portray themselves as technically competent because they are following solid and established methodological procedures as laid out by reputable intellectual predecessors and contemporaries. Statements such as "analysis followed the grounded theory approach outlined by Glaser and Strauss (1967)" that point to canonical methodological texts certainly underscore researchers' professional character. Indeed, references to the phrase *grounded theory* and its methodological vocabulary, *theoretical sampling, in vivo codes, theoretical saturation,* and so on, are among the most frequent in qualitative research (Denzin, 1994; Locke, 2001).

However, a problem arises when the references are used as "boilerplate" indicators of competence. When we invoke these or other procedures and ideas without particular knowledge, we really are using them only for the stamp of approval to legitimize our work. Essentially, we invoke these references as an impression management device vis-à-vis our reviewers in order to have our work "bask in the reflected glory" of another (Gilbert, 1977). Furthermore, without reading the originally developed work, we lose its particular contribution as we re-write its general meaning in our own work. Second, by relying so much on a few references, we miss the diversity of what constitutes qualitative research. Qualitative research constitutes a sizable umbrella under which there are many traditions. By not knowing the work we cite, we may insert references that actually offer contradictory viewpoints on how qualitative research should be conducted as well as inconsistent worldviews regarding the nature of the social realities we study. Accordingly, we confuse the methods of investigation that have been developed, and create an impression that "anything goes" in the conduct of qualitative research.

INSTITUTIONAL AND HUMAN SCIENTIST AS FIELD-KNOWLEDGEABLE STORYTELLER

An obvious and unique characteristic of qualitative research is that it is field-based. The very act of developing theorized storylines from the field story generated through our engagement with particular social settings automatically raises the questions of whether we "were there," and while there, whether we were able to experience and learn enough to allow us to understand and interpret what went on. Following the lead of anthropologists and others doing ethnographic research (Van Maanen, 1988), we often rely on this "have been there" authority to characterize ourselves as scientific in our work. Did we engage the research setting sufficiently intensively and extensively to understand the events, situations, and people we engaged? Did we observe and record in sufficiently fine detail to warrant an insightful and competent understanding of the situation studied? As we indicated in previous work (Golden-Biddle & Locke, 1993), when authors portray a detailed familiarity with the field setting and its members, they are establishing themselves as authentic or field-knowledgeable storytellers. That is, as authors we convey certain details and understandings of the field obtainable only by having "been there." Furthermore, when we write ourselves as participants in the field, we portray our human character as well as demonstrate that we were there intimately involved with the everyday lives of individuals.

By portraying familiarity with members' actions, what they do every day, authors establish their field-knowledgeable character. Gail Whiteman and William Cooper (2000), in their study of a Cree beaver trapper in Northern Quebec, establish the lead author's knowledge about the tallyman's way of life by demonstrating in detail the beaver trapper's daily routines and by portraying her at work with the trapper out in the cold:

> A section of the lake was marked with long tree poles sticking up through the snow and down through the ice. Freddy explained that the trap was positioned between the two poles on either side of the passageway into the beaver dam. The dam was under the ice and snow, not obvious at all from where we stood. Freddy told me that we had to dig out the fresh snow. I was glad that the snow was dry and light because there was a lot of it. After I'd finished digging, Freddy got the ice chisel and broke a hole through the ice to where he had set the trap a few days before. He told me to clear away the ice from the opening. . . . When I was done, Freddy poked through the hole with a long spruce branch. He said that he thought he'd caught a beaver. (p. 1270)

The mundane work involved in beaver trapping described with a detail that, for example, identifies the wood used, conveys the researcher as field knowledgeable. Similarly, when authors portray what members think about their lives in particular organizations, they also establish their field-based expertise. In the following illustration taken from a study of funeral home workers, Steve Barley reveals the staff's innermost thoughts and fears about their work: They do not want to drop the body as it is being moved from the home to the funeral parlor.

> Having positioned the onlookers away from the scene, the funeral staff moves whatever furniture is necessary to provide open access for the litter, but the path is also cleared to assure that no unwanted noise might be caused by bumping the stretcher into pieces of furniture. Noises are avoided in order to guard against, among other things, the perception that the staff has dropped the body. (from Barley, 1983, p. 407)

Kathy Charmaz conveys detailed understanding of the life situation of her research subject by portraying the thoughts and feelings surrounding intimate details of her life:

> Christine has little social life by now; her friends from high school and her bowling days have busy family and work lives. When she first became ill, Christine had some hasty encounters with several of those friends who accused her of feigning illness. She feels her isolation keenly, although all she can handle after work is resting on the couch. Her relationship with her elderly mother has never been close; she disapproves of her brother who has moved back in with their mother and is taking drugs. One continuing light in Christine's life is her recently married niece who just had a baby. (from Charmaz, 1999, p. 363)

Finally, the sense that researchers have been there and are knowledgeable is enhanced when they demonstrate insider language to make their claims. The use of colloquialisms by the Adlers in their description of the resocialization of basketball players—a key component in their framework for developing intense loyalty—illustrates this (Adler & Adler, 1988):

> No players, even the "candyasses," were immune from these tirades (from the coach).
>   . . . The coach drilled the individualistic "hot dog" qualities out of them and shaped them into team players. (p. 407)

In conclusion, when we orient our work to academic journal publication outlets, our writing depicts the character of institutional scientist, carrying the marks of the Academy. Yet, as we have indicated, within broad institutional limits, authors also provide the institutional storyteller a more individual, personal, and human character. We are not suggesting that our texts are invalid or otherwise unscientific. Nor are we suggesting that only institutional portrayals of character are constructed. Personal human depictions are equally crafted as the human scientist; both are written into being. Rather, we are making the point that our scientific products are constructed with language within the context of the institution of science (Gusfield, 1981; Knorr-Cetina, 1981; Latour & Woolgar, 1986). We have considerable flexibility, therefore, to decide who we want to be in our writing and how to develop our own character. Indeed, many seasoned researchers and scholars have done so and are recognizable through their writing. For example, Geertz (1988) discusses the highly personalized styles of eminent anthropologists as portrayed in books; Evans-Pritchard's highly visual "slide show" style being a case in point. In this respect, the creation of an individual character becomes the "writer's characteristic way of saying things" (Morner & Rausch, 1991, p. 214), or of incorporating more of the person in the writing. Our writing choices both emerge and multiply as we become increasingly conscious of how we and others convey the storyteller in journal articles.

FIVE

RE-WRITING THE STORY

Crafting a journal article is both a time-intensive and extensive process; a given paper will go through literally dozens of iterations on its way to publication. At various moments during this iterative process, it will also be viewed and influenced by different readers and audiences. Whereas till now we have focused on the work of crafting a journal article as largely an individual process, in this chapter we attend as well to the social dimension of our writing, specifically the influence exerted by our professional community on our manuscripts as they journey to publication.

What happens to the stories we tell when we present them to readers? How do audiences influence and change our stories? What role do informal audiences, for example, colleagues, play in shaping and re-writing our stories? What role do more formal audiences, such as reviewers and editors, play in re-writing our stories? How do we engage productively with these institutional gatekeepers of our publication outlets so that our manuscripts improve and strengthen as a result of their input as well as stay true to the story we want to tell?

To explore these questions, we spoke with several authors for the first and now second editions of this book who graciously took time to be interviewed about their manuscripts' journeys. They also provided us with the written "traces" of their particular review processes: original submissions, revised drafts, reviewer and editor comments, and the authors' responses to the reviewer/editor comments. Their generosity has made it possible for us to look at the journeys of thirteen different manuscripts, identified in Table 5.1.

Table 5.1   Profiled Articles

Year	Journal	Authors	Title
1991	*Administrative Science Quarterly, 36,* 245–268	Robert I. Sutton	Maintaining Norms About Expressed Emotions: The Case of Bill Collectors
1991	*Academy of Management Journal, 33,* 517–554	Jane E. Dutton & Janet Dukerich	Keeping an Eye on the Mirror: Image and Identity in Organizational Adaptation
1993	*Academy of Management Journal, 36,* 1465–1514	Robert P. Gephart	The Textual Approach: Risk and Blame in Disaster Sensemaking
1993	*MIS Quarterly* (September), pp. 309–340	Wanda Orlikowski	CASE Tools as Organizational Change: Investigating Incremental and Radical Changes in Systems Development
1995	*Academy of Management Journal, 38,* 997–1035	David Boje	Stories of the Storytelling Organization: A Postmodern Analysis of Disney as "Tamara-Land"
1996	*Organization Science, 7,* 40–59	Karen D. Locke	A Funny Thing Happened! The Management of Consumer Emotions in Service Encounters
1997	*Organization Science, 8,* 593–611	Karen Golden-Biddle & Hayagreeva Rao	Breaches in the Boardroom: Organizational Identity and Conflicts of Commitment in a Non-Profit Organization
1999	*Administrative Science Quarterly, 44,* 57–81	Leslie Perlow	The Time Famine: Toward a Sociology of Work Time
1999	*MIS Quarterly, 23,* 39–66	Geoff Walsham & Sundeep Sahay	GIS for District-Level Administration in India: Problems and Opportunities

Year	Journal	Authors	Title
2000	*Administrative Science Quarterly, 45,* 494–522	Margarete Arndt & Barbara Bigelow	Presenting Structural Innovation in an Institutional Environment: Hospitals' Use of Impression Management
2002	*Journal of Management Inquiry, 11,* 128–146	Ann Cunliffe	Social Poetics as Management Inquiry: A Dialogical Approach
2004	*Organization Science, 15,* 295–309	Martha Feldman	Resources in Emerging Structures and Processes of Change
2006	*Academy of Management Journal, 49,* 235–262	Michael Pratt, Kevin W. Rockmann, & Jeffrey B. Kaufmann	Constructing Professional Identity: The Role of Work and Identity Learning Cycles in the Customization of Identity Among Medical Residents

Based on these materials, in this chapter we share some themes about how colleagues and institutional gatekeepers participate in the re-writing of manuscripts, both prior to and during the review process.

RE-WRITING THE MANUSCRIPT PRIOR TO JOURNAL REVIEW

In our discussions with them, authors noted how early feedback of all kinds— whether received in written form by "friendly reviewers," or during invited talks, colloquia, professional conferences, or hallway conversations—influenced their developing manuscripts. Specifically, audience and readers' responses gave authors the chance to see how others reacted to and understood their developing paper; a chance to literally view their narrative through others' eyes. These responses also provided affirmation and encouragement for the writing project, as well as guidance and suggestions that challenged or highlighted particular aspects of the paper. In turn, actively considering these responses enabled authors to gain clarity about their ideas, recognize when some ideas weren't working, and become aware of what others found intriguing in their writing project. Together, their experiences highlight the importance of sharing one's work with colleagues and other audiences early and often, and recognize that writing a journal article requires others' assistance.

Several of the authors pointed to colleagues' encouraging responses to early drafts of writing—not yet in the form of a journal article—as indicating that the work might be viable as a journal submission. For example, Leslie Perlow shared that, after reading her dissertation which told the field story of her research, a senior colleague empowered her to consider developing it as an article for a highly regarded journal in the organizational studies discipline. Geoff Walsham pointed to the positive reception of an earlier conference paper on integrating actor network theory into the information systems field as an important pre-journal moment. In particular, it helped him realize that readers might consider it interesting to develop a manuscript for a special issue of a highly regarded journal in his field that brought together actor network theory and the field project he and Sundeep Sahay had conducted.

In a similar vein, Wanda Orlikowski shared that the responses of colleagues was a part of how her comparative case study of the implementation of CASE tools took shape. Her dissertation study, completed in 1988, had been an intensive field study of this technology in a software consulting firm, SCC. Two years later, she took advantage of an opportunity to conduct another study of the implementation of a similar technology in a petroleum products company, PCC. She commented that when she presented a descriptive case narrative of PCC's implementation of CASE tools at her institution's research center, she recalled "people being interested in a comparative analysis as they knew about my previous study."

In thinking about their paper, Margarete Arndt and Barbara Bigelow indicated that early on they were trying to sort through the question of whether the paper represented an original contribution to, or an application of, theory. Believing that it did make a theoretical contribution, they submitted a draft manuscript for review to a division of their professional association that focused on contribution to theory. It was accepted, and they reported that based on the responses by reviewers and those who stopped by their session to discuss the paper,

> We walked away from that with some confirmation that the paper made a substantive contribution to theory. Up to the presentation we only had each other. We can be very critical with each other, critiquing each other's thoughts. Ultimately though, it is still the two of us; this was the first time we had external validation—yes, we have something here.

In addition, once they decided on the target journal outlet, they sent the draft manuscript to two colleagues whom they trusted to challenge them; their reading gave the authors a "green light" to go ahead with the submission.

In addition to affirmation of ideas and direction, the responses of colleagues and presentation audiences also shaped the papers in particular directions by encouraging as well as directly challenging specific ideas. For example, Leslie Perlow's senior colleague advised her to make much more of the paper's core empiricized ideas captured in the "time famine" metaphor as she developed her dissertation into a journal article.

As well, Martha Feldman shared that while having a conversation with a colleague about her work, he "was pressing me on why did it matter . . . why did these routines matter." In replying to this question, she said she began to realize how the stories of bulimia were a way of showing how different resources were available for dealing with bulimia in a residence hall, depending on what routines were used to organize other aspects of the organization, like hiring of the resident staff. At that point, she remarked, "the big picture became clearer . . . and what I needed to think about was the matter of how I showed it."

In working with a large project, Mike Pratt made multiple presentations over a three-year period of successive drafts of the manuscript he and his coauthors, Kevin Rockmann and Jeffrey Kaufmann, were writing. Audience responses at these presentations helped to shape and refine the manuscript's core empiricized ideas and, though to a lesser extent, also its theoretical focus. As an illustration, he discussed how, in an early invited presentation that represented the first time they "rolled out with the ideas" of their paper, the audience challenged their initial conceptualization of their field story. In that draft, they had "the idea that people choose from different identities"—identity menus. However, they received a very negative reaction to this core empiricized idea from a respected colleague. Specifically, the feedback they got from the presentation was that the concept of identity menus "was not dynamic enough. Menus seemed very static and people were asking, 'where is the action?'" In light of this negative response, they worked on crafting a more dynamic conceptualization of multiple identities and they continued to present at colloquia. Over a three-year period, different ways of understanding the multiple identity field story were framed and presented to different audiences as "identity integrity," "identity syncretism," and "identity customization."

Martha Feldman highlighted another moment where she was giving a talk about her paper and the audience questioned her conceptualization of "resource." In particular, they kept seeing resource as a thing, and they overlooked its mutability; that is, how the way humans act creates resources. Indeed the difference between the audience's and author's understanding of resource was the central point, and the questioning responses she received helped Martha more clearly discern what she needed to do in the paper in order to make this point more accessible for readers accustomed to thinking of resources as immutable. Furthermore, in so doing, the paper ultimately was strengthened conceptually.

Although in the previous situations, the suggestions and challenges to the manuscripts are overt and explicit, reader and audience responses can also be subtle and still influential. For example, Ann Cunliffe recounts how she noticed the facial expressions of a particular audience member during a conference presentation. She recalls that he scrunched up his face at a comment she made relating to the language used by the managers in her research conversations. Specifically, she was assuming that these managers' use of language in the research situation was similar to their ways of talking in everyday work conversations. She then addressed that assumption.

Hopefully the examples described above convey the importance that these authors accorded the opportunities to gain outside perspectives on their developing manuscripts, especially but not exclusively prior to submitting the manuscript for journal review. Regardless of whether authors followed every suggestion given by readers and audience members, appreciating how others read and understood their manuscripts and what about them engendered particular responses was invaluable to making them stronger. A comment by Leslie Perlow underscored this point:

> I am a big believer in getting feedback on the paper—and doing a number of revisions before sending it in. One doesn't always have to agree with the feedback; but, usually each person has something to add that, when you step back and consider why they are giving you that feedback, it will make the paper stronger.

RE-WRITING THE MANUSCRIPT
DURING THE JOURNAL REVIEW PROCESS

As noted by Beyer, Chanove, and Fox (1995), an important characteristic of manuscripts' receiving a "revise and resubmit" decision is that reviewers become actively involved in trying to improve them. Reviewers regard submitted manuscripts as works in process and the central responsibility of their role as providing "the author with direction for enhancing" the informative value of the work to the organization studies community (Rousseau, 1995:152). This responsibility is particularly evident in "Keeping an Eye on the Mirror: Image and Identity in Organizational Adaptation" by Jane Dutton and Janet Dukerich, the paper in this group that changed the least in the review process. From the original submission, it was clear that the editor and reviewers viewed the manuscript favorably, as indicated in comments such as, "your rather lovely paper" and "I enjoyed your paper." Indeed, the editor characterized the original submission as having established the basic foundation for the paper. Yet, even with these very positive responses, the paper nevertheless went through two more revisions, which the editor described as directed at developing and strengthening what already had been accomplished in the original submission.

Indeed, an intriguing dilemma created by reviewers' and editors' engagement with the manuscript is that, on the one hand, it leads to their support, while on the other, it evokes greater involvement in suggesting changes to, and directing the revision of, the manuscript. With the exception of Bob Sutton's article, "Maintaining Norms About Expressed Emotions: The Case of Bill Collectors," whose editor strongly directed the revision, all of these papers went through at least two revisions before final acceptance. At least three other manuscripts went through revisions at other journals, prior to being submitted to the journal of publication. And the work, "Stories of the Storytelling Organization: A Post Modern Analysis of Disney as 'Tamara Land,'" by David Boje underwent five revisions at one journal prior to its publication.

Although there are several ways that institutional gatekeepers become involved in manuscripts during the formal review process, three emerged in our analyses as especially significant. First, the field story, and their reading of what it is about, engages reviewers and editors. Second, reviewers and editors direct their comments toward strengthening the theorized storyline by drawing on their understanding of its potentially most significant contribution. Finally, authors are active in their responses to reviewer comments, seeking to be responsive to suggestions for development, while trying to stay true to what they see as the story and contribution of their manuscript.

Engaging and Re-Writing the Field Story and What It Is About

Certainly the field story, with its attendant glimpses of organizational life, constitutes one of the attractions of qualitative manuscripts. Indeed, in several of the studies we profile in this chapter, editors and reviewers were clearly engaged by the field narrative. For example, one of Bob Sutton's reviewers was especially curious about the study's setting: credit rating companies. This reviewer commented,

> This paper offers a fascinating view into a world often regarded as mysterious and intriguing. In our current society, the prediction that Big Brother would be watching us has often come to be translated into the activities of the credit rating companies, with their expansive reach into nearly complete knowledge of our activities. These bill collectors form one arm of that gigantic system.

Furthermore, the editor highlighted this interest in the cover letter:

> As the reviewers remarked, this is a fascinating peep into the workings of a mysterious occupational curiosity—the bill collector. And while the show doesn't have quite the elegance of *A Taxing Woman,* the material is reasonably detailed and provocative.

Similarly, in another example, below, the reviewer comments indicate engagement with the details of medical life expressed in "Constructing Professional Identity: The Role of Work and Identity Learning Cycles in the Customization of Identity Among Medical Residents," the study by Mike Pratt, Kevin Rockmann, and Jeffrey Kaufmann.

> What is really intriguing for me about your study is the data you have about *how* physicians develop such a strong and enduring professional identity. What I see is that surgeons throughout the world seem to act and think very similarly. The same is true for radiologists, and other specialists. It might be somewhat less true of primary care physicians—but there is still great similarity for them as well. How is such a strong identity created? The residents in your study fussed and fumed about many of the tasks they were required to do—and yet they will turn around and teach the next generation of residents in almost exactly the same way. I think you have some real insights to share about this incredible process.

In the case of David Boje's article, the editor remarked on a personal interest in the study of Disney:

> I found the general story of Disney leadership to be interesting. Perhaps, this is because I grew up at a time when Disney was "king." Furthermore, the general historical data and background are interesting.

As well, the consulting editor on Jane Dutton and Janet Dukerich's study of how the Port Authority dealt with the issue of homelessness remarked,

> The reviewers of the paper are very attracted to the issues you are addressing . . . and to the empirical setting which you have selected to study the problem.

Intriguingly, while the richness of the field story, represented in highly detailed and contextualized accounts of the comings and goings of organizational life, is a source of attraction and engages reviewers, this same richness carries an attendant liability that may become a basis for different potential re-writings of the manuscript. Specifically, qualitative data and the field stories we construct from them are multivocal. The strength of this multivocality is that the crafted field stories express the richness and complexity of real-life interactions and events. The downside of this multivocality is its inconsistency with the understood task in writing journal articles of articulating a single theorized storyline. Accordingly, when faced with multivocality expressed in the field story, the responses by reviewers and editors are likely to focus on narrowing and selecting core ideas. Thus, selection almost always results in the need to significantly re-write the manuscript. The following comments by Bob Sutton's editor emphasize this selection process in light of an interesting field story, and indicate the options that the editor saw (and preferred) in the manuscript.

> A most severely limiting feature is that the exact contribution being pursued with these observations is not clearly articulated for the reader, and perhaps not clear for the author. Especially unclear is the purpose being pursued for an audience of organizational scientists. The paper appears to be pursuing several goals at once. (1) A description of the functioning of a credit card collection organization; (2) a theory of motivation for debt repayment; (3) a set of your own and your respondents' theories about the impact of collectors' tactics in influencing debtors; (4) a theory about how collectors control their personal emotions to maintain control in a conversation with debtors. All but the first of these has little to do with organizations per se. . . . Regardless, there appears to be too many goals being pursued within the confines of a single study. Thus, as a first recommendation towards revision, we recommend that you try to focus your project to a more singular and coherent objective relevant to organizational social science. . . . You can of course pursue any of these themes. But a single short paper cannot hold up to the burden of pursuing them all simultaneously. Thus we recommend that you take a firm choice about one of these themes and forget the others for the sake of this presentation.

At the same time as multivocality is responded to at the level of the field story, of course, as the above editor comments indicate, a paper's theoretical contribution with its attendant theorized storyline is also implicated. Accordingly, the rich field story can point to one of a number of possible theoretical explanations, and thus have ramifications for the paper's potential theoretical contribution (Campbell, 1975; Gephart, 2004). The reflections of a reviewer on the findings developed in the article by Karen Locke, "A Funny Thing Happened! The Management of Consumer Emotions in Service Encounters," underscores just how multivocal our data can be in terms of their relevance for various theoretical contributions. This reviewer commented,

> However there are available empirical findings as well as conceptualizations that relate to your analyses, and I think it would greatly enrich the contribution of this paper if you were to incorporate them . . . I suspect it will also enrich your ability to analyze your data if you were to scan related conceptualizations and consider their implications for these data. For example, the discussion of the Sociability act could benefit from the literature on socialization, on first impressions and first encounters (Goffman's work), and on the establishment of rapport (such as the interviewing literature). Similarly, the establishment of master in the Mastery act may be related to the establishment of professionalism or of proficiency. . . . Parents' and clients' cooperation with the Celebratory acts (page 25) seems, in part, to relate to the norm of reciprocity, or to the contagion effect (when other people laugh it's hard not to laugh). I don't know that anyone has proposed comedy or humor in these contexts, but making the link to a broader literature is important.

In addition to the manuscript's positioning with regard to theoretical contributions on emotions, service encounters, and humor and play, this reviewer highlights a number of other literatures that may also bear on the study's findings. The choices can be overwhelming. From the editors' and reviewers' perspective, though, that choice is delimited by what they understand to be those ideas that have the greatest potential to advance theorizing and thus make a distinct contribution. This should direct the re-writing project. This is emphasized in the following reviewer comments about "Breaches in the Boardroom: Organizational Identity and Conflicts of Commitment in a Non-Profit Organization," addressed to Karen Golden-Biddle and Huggy Rao, that enjoin them to narrow the field story expressed in their data and create a theorized storyline that will provide for the greatest theoretical contribution.

It is my judgment that the findings are stated too broadly and too generally. The paper needs more focus and the data need to be organized in a more compelling way around this focus. . . . Currently your work supports a lot of ideas that are fairly well-known (and thus the data illustrates another application of these ideas), as well as introducing other ideas that are less well understood, provocative, and I think important. I'll try to isolate what I see as claims falling into each of these categories. In doing this, my hope is that you can adjust the focus of the paper and the discussion of your research to highlight claims which fit the later category. I think this is where your work adds really important insights.

These comments underscore the need to emphasize the portions of the field story that offer less well-understood, provocative ideas. The more familiar ideas, then, should be erased.

Re-Writing the Articulated Theorized Storylines

In these manuscripts, there was extensive attention on the part of reviewers and editors to the theorized storylines and their development (as compared with the field stories or data themselves). As institutional gatekeepers, they are most concerned with how the field and academic worlds are brought together to construct the manuscript's disciplinary contribution. Thus, they focus on delimiting and strengthening the theorized storyline that is offered in the manuscript and on identifying possible alternative storylines with greater potential for theoretical contribution. Consider these editorial comments regarding "Presenting Structural Innovation in an Institutional Environment: Hospitals' Use of Impression Management," Margarete Arndt and Barbara Bigelow's submission:

There are concerns about the clarity of the theoretical contribution your study makes. In other words, although there is general consensus among the reviewers that the paper is very interesting, whether or not it significantly breaks new ground or pushes thinking with respect to either institutional theory research or impression management research is somewhat less clear.

This focus on theory and theorized storyline is not surprising: The review process calls for re-writing the theorized storyline in some respect. As developed in Chapter 1, disciplinary readers in science are interested in details or "facts" provided by our data, primarily as illustrations of theory or points of view (Langer, 1964). It is their significance that matters; their significance to the theoretical streams of work. What the data mean and especially what theoretical import they signify are arenas of dialogue, often the most disputed in a discipline and, consequently, an area of great attention in the review process. Thus, our authors noted that by and large it was the "front" and "back" sections— that is, the theoretical framing and implications of the field story—that were the object of most significant reviewer and editor attention throughout the review process—and that were substantially re-written through the revision process.

We get a first glance at the process of re-writing theorized storylines by looking at how the titles of these manuscripts changed from original submission to final acceptance. Table 5.2 details these changes for the 13 profiled manuscripts. With the exception of the articles by Jane Dutton and Janet Dukerich, and Walsham and Sahay, the titles changed along the way. In the case of David Boje's article, the title changed five times.

In this section, we profile a number of examples illustrating how reviewers and editors engaged authors to re-write the theorized storylines offered in the manuscript. In most cases, they acted in their comments to question, probe, or clarify how the authors had brought together the worlds of field and theory. For example, they offered suggestions for authors to highlight a particular aspect of theorizing over another in further developing the manuscript, and questioned whether or how the represented data supported theoretical claims. Occasionally, they also identified storylines not considered or offered in the original manuscript but that they suggested might hold greater theoretical promise.

A manuscript journey that shows the room available, even during the formal review process, for significant honing and resolving the field story's significance into a theorized storyline is "Constructing Professional Identity: The Role of Work and Identity Learning Cycles in the Customization of Identity Among Medical Residents." Mike Pratt shared that this was a huge study involving six years of data collection, and he and his coauthors "struggled with how to frame it." As noted in the discussion of audience response prior to journal submission, the core empiricized idea from this research initially centered on the notion of multiple identities in the field story. But when, through the process of working that idea and shaping it into a theorized storyline, the emphasis on multiplicity gave way to a concern with how identity was constructed, the theoretical framing also changed.

Their initial working paper articulated the core idea of identity menus and marshaled it to support a theorized storyline about socialization. As the authors

Table 5.2   Title Changes

Authors	Title at Journal Submission	Title at Journal Acceptance
Arndt & Bigelow	The Use of Impression Management in the Presentation of Structural Innovation	Presenting Structural Innovation in an Institutional Environment: Hospitals' Use of Impression Management
	New title with first resubmission: The Presentation of Structural Innovation in an Institutional Environment	
Boje	A Postmodern Analysis of Disney Leadership: The Story of Storytelling Organization Succession From Feudal Bureaucratic to "Tamara-Land" Discourses	Stories of the Storytelling Organization: A Postmodern Analysis of Disney as "Tamara-Land"
Cunliffe	Every Day Conversations: A Social Poetics of Managing	Social Poetics as Management Inquiry: A Dialogical Approach
Dutton & Dukerich	Keeping an Eye on the Mirror: Image and Identity in Organizational Adaptation	Keeping an Eye on the Mirror: Image and Identity in Organizational Adaptation
Feldman	Resources in Emerging Structures and Change Processes	Resources in Emerging Structures and Processes of Change
	Redesigning Work Practices and Employee Empowerment: An Approach to a Managerial Dilemma (*earlier version submitted to policy journal*)	
Gephart	Public Inquiry as Performance Occasion: Tracking the Myth of Organization	The Textual Approach: Risk and Blame in Disaster Sensemaking
Golden-Biddle & Rao	Monitoring as Ritual: A Study of Faith and Facework in Non-Profit Boards	Breaches in the Boardroom: Organizational Identity and Conflicts of Commitment in a Non-Profit Organization

(Continued)

(Continued)

Authors	Title at Journal Submission	Title at Journal Acceptance
Locke	Emotion Management in Professional Relationships: A Study of Comedic Microperformances	A Funny Thing Happened! The Management of Consumer Emotions in Service Encounters
Orlikowski	Incremental and Radical Changes in Systems Development: Investigating the Organizational Implications of CASE Tools	CASE Tools as Organizational Change: Investigating Incremental and Radical Changes in Systems Development
Perlow	The Time Famine: Towards a Sociology of Work Time *New title with first resubmission*: Time Use at Work: A Case Study of Knowledge Workers	The Time Famine: Toward a Sociology of Work Time
Pratt, Rockmann, & Kaufmann	Identity Customization at Work Socialization, Multiple Identities and Identity Customization: Towards a Model of Work Identity Integrity *(earlier version submitted to different journal)*	Constructing Professional Identity: The Role of Work and Identity Learning Cycles in the Customization of Identity Among Medical Residents
Sutton	Getting the Money: Bill Collectors' Expressed Emotions as Tools of Social Influence Over Debtors	Maintaining Norms About Expressed Emotions: The Case of Bill Collectors
Walsham & Sahay	GIS for District-Level Administration in India: Problems and Opportunities	GIS for District-Level Administration in India: Problems and Opportunities

explained, "Since we were invited to study physician training, we were immersed in the socialization literature, which usually talks about being socialized into a single role. But we know life is more complicated than that." Thus the core empiricized idea about multiple identities was initially part of a theorized storyline regarding the messiness of socialization. The introductory lines of their working paper read,

Social groups, such as professions and organizations, rely on the socialization of members for their continued existence. It is this transmission of values, beliefs, and skills to new members that allows organizations such as IBM and Disney to retain their "identity" over time. Socialization also influences how organizational members view themselves, and thus plays a central role in forming and maintaining the "identity" of individuals.

In the final re-visioning of the manuscript, the core empiricized ideas shift, centering on the "identity customization processes," and it is crafted into a theorized story line about the construction of professional identity. Accordingly, the first line of the published version reads,

> Despite a growing interest in matters of "identity" in organizational studies, we know relatively little about how identities are formed among those who carry out some of the most critical organizational functions: professionals (Ibarra, 1999).

Following a journal submission in which the manuscript did not advance, the authors realized that the framing as a story about socialization was not working and they began trying out different theoretical possibilities. At the next journal location, the paper's theorized storyline pulled together a core empiricized idea of identity customization and integrated it into a literature synthesized to highlight identity construction processes in organizations. The reviewers, however, were unsatisfied, pushing the authors to reshape their storyline more cogently and to highlight its particular contribution. Thus one reviewer commented,

> The core storyline of the paper is not yet clear. There are too many subplots and by ways (e.g. the model of identity construction which does not really lead anywhere; the three forms of identity customization which needs to be theorized more). My own reading suggests that the crunch conclusion at the end of the article is that that member led identity construction processes were more evident than multiple identity management processes or identity trans-forming organizations, both of which perspectives have been held up by the literature. If this is correct, then the initial literature review (pp. 3–7) could be more focused around these three different perspectives so as to set up the debate. . . . The paper needs reworking to ensure that the core added value is clearer and then working back from that, to ensure that the paper tells a clear story which leads to a well substantiated theoretical and empirical addition.

Another reviewer argued strongly for the direction the refinement should take:

I think that your paper is about how individuals develop a professional identity. And I think this is very important and very interesting. Sometimes in your writing, you say "professional identity" and other times you seem to suggest that your study is about identity more generally. You point out (p 8) that you selected physicians to study because they are an extreme case. This has both pluses and minuses. Although you will find various arguments about who is really a professional, you will seldom find an argument about whether physicians are professionals. What I'm suggesting here is that I think you have a case that is relevant for professional identity, and your study itself should stick within these boundaries. You might make suggestions in your conclusions about how relevant your findings are for other workers—but your focus should be on professionals.

Mike Pratt highlighted the significance of this response; he remarked:

Those reviewers were really useful because they said it's not about multiple identities and socialization. Rather this is a great story about how professionals form their identity—this was a big figure ground flip—once we abandoned that everything seemed to fall in place.

With this, some three years after their initial conference presentation of the manuscript, the paper had its narrowed and focused theorized storyline. The identities of professionals had, of course, always been embedded in this paper, but through engagement with the reviewers it was selected and accorded the greatest theoretical salience. As a result, the authors had to significantly extend the reading they had done to include the literature on professions in order to re-write the final version's intertextual field to locate their contribution.

Another manuscript journey showing a different re-crafting of the theorized storyline is "The Time Famine: Toward a Sociology of Work Time" by Leslie Perlow. This manuscript originally offered its contribution as a "sociology of work time," but in response to the first set of reviewer comments, moved away from this while honing and theorizing its core empiricized idea of how people collectively use time at work. The comments by reviewers and editor prompted this effort, as they were unanimous that the paper needed significant theoretical development, a point summarized by the editor.

A successful revision will entail a major effort on your part, particularly in the area of theoretical development. Our current judgment is that you have made a good first effort at conceptualizing and investigating the collective nature of time management, but more work needs to be done before we can be confident that the results provide a significant theoretical contribution . . .

As the manuscript is currently written, a great deal of space is devoted to the practical implications . . . and the qualitative account. The theory, what you have labeled the sociology of work time, seems to be tacked on at the end . . . You need to keep in mind that [this journal's] readers are less interested in the specifics of engineering software than they are in the implications of this research for organization theory. The more relevant criterion for publication . . . is whether any research makes a significant theoretical contribution . . .

The reviewers also provided a number of suggested articles and research streams to incorporate. In revising the manuscript, Leslie deleted the metaphor of time famine and the conceptual framing of sociology of work time. As well, she constructed a new theoretical location for the study using the reviewers' suggestions, represented in a new title: "Time Use at Work: A Case Study of Knowledge Workers." This re-written storyline theorized the field story as "a study of time use at work," and grounded it in a synthesized construction of a "time use" literature that highlighted the gap addressed.

The existing literature on time use contributes to at least a partial under-standing of both how and why individuals do and should spend their time at work. However, three additional components are necessary to understand the use of time at work, especially among knowledge workers. The interdependency of work patterns, the enactment of these patterns, and their effective-ness, particularly at the level of the collective, must each be considered.

The additional components representing the gap in time use research were then used as organizing devices for the data. That is, the field story was now represented in the manuscript according to theoretical categories, or the "three additional components necessary to understand time use at work": interdependent work patterns, enactment of work patterns, and effectiveness of work patterns.

Intriguingly, after the second round of reviews the editor provisionally accepted the manuscript, but indicated that the theory still required some development. In particular, the editor noted that in re-writing the theorized storyline, some aspect of the contribution may have been lost:

I am still searching for the illusive theoretical contribution that distinguishes this paper as publishable in [this journal]. On this last point, I found myself going back to the original submission to try to understand what had been lost, and added, during the revision process. I concluded that the "sociology of work time" had provided the initial conceptual promise that was missing from the revision. Thus, somewhere between the original submission and the revision is the publishable manuscript . . .

In describing her or his suggestions, the editor suggested that the title change to the paper might represent what was lost in the review process and point to what needed to be brought back in.

I would like to begin with the title of the paper, because I feel it is symptomatic of the changes that you made. The new title reflects an emphasis on knowledge work rather than the notion of time famine and the sociology of work time. Although this is a case of knowledge workers, I do not feel that knowledge work is the main focus, or contribution, of the paper. These knowledge workers simply represent the sample you investigated . . . I felt that the shortage of time and explaining this shortage by systematically and simultaneously considering all the elements of your "sociology of work time" framework was the main focus. As you wrote in the original, "I, on the other hand, study individuals' use of time as a means to explore why they suffer from a syndrome of having too much to do and not enough time to do it." I thought this sentence nicely summarized the motivation for your research . . .

In her letter to the editor, Leslie agreed that the changes to the manuscript were reflected in the new title, and in the final version, decided to return to the earlier title. As well, Leslie indicated that she was "delighted" with the suggestions, and reintegrated both sociology of work time and the metaphor, time famine. These changes did not, however, eliminate the revised focus on a study of time use or significantly alter the revised theoretical location. Rather, it provided an overarching framing within which Leslie's now re-crafted storyline assumed greater theoretical significance.

Three shorter examples depict other ways that reviewers and editors can suggest re-writing the theorized storyline. For example, comments can illuminate potential ways to deepen the connection between the field story and the theorized storyline developed by the author in the manuscript. We see this in Martha Feldman's paper, "Resources in Emerging Structures and Processes of Change," when a reviewer indicates there might be a "mismatch" between what they found insightful in their reading and the proposed theoretical framing. These comments are profiled below.

While I found the details of the case interesting and the insights on the changing nature of resources (from the building directors' point of view) compelling, I would have liked to see a deeper development of the link between the data and the structuration theory framing (that to me was covered rather briefly on pgs. 25–26) . . . Part of the problem that I had with the paper might have to do with a mismatch between what I found insightful in the paper and the overall framing of the paper. To me, the unexpected changes in the composition of resources as a result of the change in routines (and the consequences wrought by this change) seemed to be the interesting finding of the paper. The linkage of this finding to structuration theory seemed a little more tenuous. Could such a process of unexpected change be wrought by more traditional theories of change (i.e., punctuated equilibrium, incremental) or is a structurational lens more appropriate? I suspect it is, given its emphasis on the emergent nature of change espoused by this theory, but this needs to be made clearer to the reader.

Alternatively, comments can point to theorized storylines not considered originally by the author(s) or explicitly offered in the manuscript. This is the case, for example, when reviewer/editorial comments re-position the study and its storyline into a different intertextual field. We see this in the paper by Karen Golden-Biddle and Huggy Rao, "Conflicts in the Boardroom: Organizational Identity and Conflicts of Commitment in a Non-Profit Organization," when a reviewer questioned the original basis of the paper in institutional theory, proposing instead that the conversation on impression management might be a more appropriate partner with agency theory. These comments are excerpted below.

This is a well-written paper that shows clear understanding of institutional theory. The paper is ambitious in seeking to provide thick descriptions of the relations between directors and top managers, and thus clarify principal/agent relations. The paper also seeks to provide insight on the impression management of conflict events. Perhaps because of the ambitious nature of the project, the contribution to any one of the above mentioned literatures is not always clear. For example, at the end of the paper, I still wasn't clear whether, in the authors' view, the data supported the view of boards as "pliant pawns or vigilant monitors" (p. 4). How does this study relate back to the agency theory literature that frames the opening of the paper? . . . then later . . . the institutional framing of the paper seems inappropriate. . . . A more promising perspective is impression management, and here the conjunction of agency theory with impression management mentioned in the discussion is a potential contribution.

Or, as our final example shows, reviewers for a special journal issue can suggest re-writing associated with the issue focus. In "The Textual Approach: Risk and Blame in Disaster Sensemaking," Bob Gephart intended to theorize notions of managerial control and organization as fragile and illusory through the story of the gas-line explosion that resulted in the deaths of two men. However, as part of a special issue forum that was intended to highlight configural approaches to organization, the review process identified the methods by which the story was disclosed as most interesting. When the theorized story was re-written, it focused on the use of the textual approach in organizational analysis. The story of the disaster was subordinated to the study's methodological story, and the idea that organization itself is a myth disappeared from the manuscript.

The examples above show that, while authors offer theorized storylines in the original submission for journal review, editors and reviewers bring their own apprehensions of the literature, as well as their own ideas as to how to re-craft the storyline to strengthen the manuscript's disciplinary contribution. Thus, the intertextual fields that the broader audience of organizational scholars read in the published work and their connections with particular field stories are actively constructed and re-constructed in the interactions between gatekeepers and authors. The various re-writings of the manuscript represent these interactions. The final construction of the theorized storyline, then, is a negotiated outcome concerning what constitutes the most significant connection between the field and academic worlds; between the possible intertextual locations and the field data. Through this process, the reviewers do participate in re-writing the positioning of our studies.

How Authors Engage Reviewer
Suggestions for Re-Writing the Manuscript

In examining how authors engage the challenges and suggestions made by editors and reviewers for re-writing their submitted manuscripts, we see that they navigated a delicate and sometimes tension-filled space. On the one hand, authors sought to be responsive to reviewers' and editors' suggestions for development. So, for example, they took care to acknowledge the weaknesses pointed out in the review process and engaged in often substantial re-working of the manuscript to address them. On the other hand, authors needed to establish boundaries around the direction they were willing to take in re-writing their manuscript. Rather than accepting all comments, they had to discern for example which comments offered by reviewers and editors brought forward the most potential in the manuscript. Thus, authors needed at once to carefully and mindfully consider the challenges, suggestions, and directions offered by reviewers and editors while identifying and clarifying the particular boundaries required to sustain authorial control of and stay true to their vision for the paper.

Margarete Arndt and Barbara Bigelow described their engagement with the reviewers and the boundaries they drew in the process in the following terms:

> [We] are really careful to do whatever reviewers say that seems reasonable and does not alter the basic paper we want to submit. When something comes back in a review, and we say the reviewers didn't get it, then we think that we didn't make it clear.

In the instance of "Presenting Structural Innovation in an Institutional Environment: Hospitals' Use of Impression Management," the core empiricized idea—that the clinical and medical facilities studied used different impression management techniques with different innovations relative to legitimacy—was realized and established prior to the manuscript's being presented as a conference paper or going out for friendly review. The authors also understood that in these innovations they were looking at fundamental building blocks in institutional fields, and that an examination of structural innovation constituted a gap in institutional literature. Thus all the elements from which to fashion a theorized storyline were in place. When the manuscript was submitted for review, however, the reviewers' and editor's readings of the manuscript reflected an understanding of its theorized storyline as centered in impression management theory. Thus, the editor expressed concern about the manuscript's theoretical contribution in impression management, raising the issue repeatedly in the letter, indicating specifically,

> I had some concerns about the extent to which the paper adds to our knowledge about organization impression management.
>
> . . . relatively little is really said about impression management theory in depth as a way of setting up the qualitative study that follows . . .
>
> [noting the examples of strategies presented in the paper] reflect relatively well-known and well-understood impression management strategies . . .
>
> [concluding] there is a need for a stronger, more theory-oriented introduction that more compellingly ties impression management theory to the institutional argument.

Barbara Bigelow noted that being confronted with this strong direction to further develop the manuscript's articulation of impression management theory was for her the "most meaningful moment." She continued,

> The title of the paper was, "The Use of Impression Management in the Presentation of Structural Innovation." . . . What they [the editor and reviewers] wanted to know was, "what was your contribution to impression management?" And we realized that we were not making a contribution to impression management; we were making a contribution to institutional theory. This put us in an interesting position because what we had to do was to write back and say we are not going to do what you asked . . . if we did then it wouldn't be the same paper, and not the paper we wanted to write.

Indeed, in the letter accompanying and describing their revisions, she and Margarete explained,

> We feel that the previous version of our paper created expectations concerning contributions to impression management that our research was not intended to address. Our original intention was to extend institutional theory. We used categories of impression management to code our data for conceptual as well as contextual reasons, based on extant research . . . however, our research was not designed to extend impression management theory. We regret that we created those expectations and have addressed the situation by changing the title of the paper and by focusing the contribution section exclusively on the implications for institutional theory.

It is important to note that while the authors resisted this direction, it nevertheless contributed to the re-crafting and re-writing of the manuscript. In the face of the editor and reviewer comments regarding impression management, they appreciated that their contribution to institutional theory was not sufficiently strong either, especially as one of the reviewers had raised questions regarding the distinction between neo and old institutional theory, which they had not addressed. So they went back and re-read and did additional work to make their arguments about institutional theory stronger. In so doing, they realized that, in fact, they had a more significant contribution to make integrating "neo" and "old" institutional perspectives. They remarked, "In sticking with our placement in institutional theory [instead of switching to impression management] we were able actually to extend its contribution there."

In the instance of "CASE Tools as Organizational Change: Investigating Incremental and Radical changes in Systems Development," Wanda

Orlikowski's engagement was complicated by the status of the manuscript as one of the journal's first published wholly inductive qualitative studies. It was the practice of this journal at the time to send articles to both academics and practitioners and, indeed, the manuscript went to six reviewers, one of whom was a practitioner. The author reflected that while "I knew there would be more than the customary three, I don't think I expected six." The reviewers' challenges generally focused on two areas; theoretical contribution and the implications of the paper's methodology on the core theorized ideas.

As initially submitted, the paper's articulated contribution lay in challenging an existing assumption that the adoption of CASE tools will lead to predictable outcomes and offering in its place "a specification of the various circumstances within which certain outcomes are more likely." In the face of multiple reviewer challenges to the significance of this contribution, the associate editor suggested that the author build a much stronger case for the manuscript's significance by documenting and explaining at length the implicit assumptions present in the literature so that the study's challenge to them would stand in sharper relief. While acknowledging that the contribution needed to be addressed, Wanda explained that the strategy of demonstrating what was implicit turned out in practice to be "cumbersome and . . . unsatisfactory as a powerful argument." Instead she chose a shift in focus, making figural the organizational change aspect of her field story and suggesting "the value of conceptualizing the introduction of CASE tools as a form of organizational change." As she argued in her response to the associate editor,

> I believe that this is an important message for the IS research and practice community . . . The lens of organizational change allows consideration of actors' strategic conduct, the social context, and process of adoption and use around CASE tools, elements which I had argued were missing from prior studies. While I could not demonstrate conclusively the questionable implicit assumptions made by this previous work, I believe that the reframing of the paper illustrates (by comparison) what has been absent from such work, and why—by considering these elements as I do in the field sites—we get a different understanding of what happens when CASE tools are introduced into organizations.

As regards the methodologically based challenges to the manuscript's core empiricized ideas, four of the six reviewers read the manuscript in positivist terms, looking for Wanda to re-write the paper so that it would contain "predictions," "more variables and contingencies," "controlled factors" and "numbers." For example, one advised, "it would be better that author(s) had some predictions in mind based on theory (there are many) before collecting any data and then use this field data to either confirm or disconfirm the hypothesis." Recognizing that these challenges came from a positivist reading of the research, the associate editor nevertheless detailed three case study choices that could be pursued in the paper's revision: wholly inductive or interpretive, deductive, or a combined approach. In sticking with the first choice, in her letter to the associate editor, Wanda explained:

> Thank you for your detailed suggestions about how to think about revising the paper. I found them very useful in helping me assess my options. While the various suggestions were all interesting, I decided to stay with the original intention of the studies, which was to do interpretive research using qualitative data and generating rich insights. I appreciate this is the more risky strategy—as you point out, such work is more difficult to present to an IS audience—however, I feel that this situation will never change unless we keep trying to present and publish interpretive research and perhaps influence people's understanding and appreciation of this approach.

As well, she affirmed the inductive nature of her study, bounding off issues inconsistent with this approach. For example, one of the reviewers raised the following issues that the paper needed to address.

> [The field story did] very little to show the unique contribution of each to change and the possible interaction effects of locus of change and nature of change on the adoption process. For example, is a process change more or less important than a product change in the adoption process? Is there a universal answer to this question? If not, what are the contingencies (i.e. moderating variables—an underdeveloped issue in this work) that count?

In her response, Wanda maintained:

> The two field studies I conducted, while able to yield certain kinds of rich findings, also cannot provide others. Thus, I am unable to answer questions such as "is a process change more or less important than a product change in the adoption process?" . . . Further, the nature of interpretive work, while it can yield grounded theory, as I do here, does not generate theory of the positivist variety, i.e., consisting of testable hypotheses with distinct independent, dependent, and moderating variables. Interpretive theory is contextual, processual, and focused on individual sensemaking and action. Its aim is to explain underlying patterns concerning social phenomena.

While she held firm to the inductive and theory building approach she had selected for this research, the manuscript was re-crafted to explain in more detail the methodological approach used.

With regards to Jane Dutton and Janet Dukerich's manuscript, "Keeping an Eye on the Mirror: Image and Identity in Organizational Adaptation," a reviewer acknowledges the location of the paper in the literature on adaptation, but sees an additional theoretical conversation for the paper to join. In this case, however, the authors choose not to incorporate the reviewer's suggestion, and explain why in their response.

> Reviewer: I see that your paper ties into adaptation as the central theoretical thrust of the paper. However, clearly learning is also a broad theoretical issue which is implicitly addressed by your data. I think that you have really under-exploited the possibilities of your data for linkages to learning. You probably don't have the space to address this topic. But, if you can, you should, or write your follow-up paper.
>
> Authors' response: We are very limited in our ability to do this, given the space limitations and the additional text that we have added in the image and identity sections. We hope that you will find the revised discussion and implications section does a better job of addressing the question of "So what is new here?," particularly in relation to what has been done in the adaptation literature. We decided after some debate, that we really did not have room to link explicitly to the learning literature . . .

Here, the authors' response indicated that, primarily due to space limitations, they could not exploit their study's implications for the conversation on organizational learning, and thus they chose to decline the invitation to write this literature into their study.

In the case of "Resources in Emerging Structures and Processes of Change," we see how Martha Feldman both reconsiders original points in light of reviewer comments, and also selects those comments that best assist her in seeing and developing the points she wants to make in light of her field story. We begin with the editor's letter, which conveyed that a revision would need to address the issue of resources (one of three issues to address), clarifying how she used the concept. Part of this letter is excerpted below.

> The . . . outside reviewers were all in substantial agreement about this manuscript. They all found it potentially important work whose subject matter is appropriate for [this journal], as do I. . . . The paper would be strengthened by providing clearer, explicit definitions, and by a deeper presentation of

related prior work. Defining and using consistently "resources" is one of the most essential tasks if you retain the current focus.

As well, all three reviewers requested further discussion and clarification of "resource," including its relationship with routines and rules, other concepts used in the paper. Two reviewers in particular pushed more specifically on the importance of clarifying resource in light of structuration theory, the theoretical location of this paper. Reviewer 1 noted, for example:

> I know there are extensive explanations of resources in Giddens and in other places, so please include a clear summary of what you mean by resources as the idea is used . . . on p. 5, rather than assert that others have used the idea of resources in a certain way, explain that use and its usefulness for your issue. Up to this point, I have no idea what a resource is as you define it, even though I am vaguely familiar with Giddens' discussion of the idea . . . on p. 27 . . . you still seem to slip back and forth between routines and resources, so if they are really the same thing, explain; if not, explain the difference.

In her response to this reviewer, Martha noted the comment's assistance in helping her think through the revision of the manuscript. She specifies resource more precisely, including defining what and when something becomes a resource. Finally, she distinguishes resource from routine and clarifies connections between her work and structuration theory.

> This was a very useful comment and made me realize that I had to make some choices. I decided to focus specifically on resources and providing a different way of understanding what resources are and the role they play in change. I have used the definition of resource provided by Sewell (1992): a source of power in interactions. This definition helps me to focus on the use of resources and to make the point that an asset or quality does not become a resource until used. Routines are patterns of action. Actions create and recreate structure (of which resources are a component) and actions are constrained and enabled by structure. One could presumably look at other forms of institutionalized action, but as much work is accomplished through organizational routines, it makes sense to use them as examples . . . I have a lengthy section in the beginning of the paper (pages 5–7) that locates resources in the social practice literature. Resources are sources of power in interactions. They are also part of the structural component of structuration, defined by Giddens as rule-resource sets.
>
>   . . . I realized that I was not very clear about what is a resource and when it is a resource. I have done several things to remedy these confusions. I've

defined resources. I've been very clear about what assets and qualities in the case become resources in the context of the example used to illustrate the relationship between schemas, actions and resources. I've provided diagrams that show both the theoretical relationships and the specific resources, schemas and actions that took place in the specific instance I use to illustrate the relationship.

In addressing reviewers' concerns about the ambiguity of "resources" in the earlier version, Martha conveys her agreement with many of the reviewers' suggestions, and specifies how she incorporates them into the revision. But she also selects which comments best assist the development of her points. We draw again on the example of resources. In this case, Reviewer 2 suggests that Martha incorporate an area into her discussion of resources—ideology and issues of signification—that was not so prevalent in the first version. Reviewer 2 commented,

> Although I think it is reasonable to focus on the social production of resources and on how these alter the structure of routines, I couldn't help but wonder if systems of signification didn't play a very important role in the case you present. . . . At any rate, you might consider at least discussing the role that ideology plays in this particular setting since it is a crucial tool that actors in your story use in the production of ongoing actions and in the lodging of warrants.

Replying to this reviewer, Martha bounds what about the concept, resource, she will develop in this paper by assessing its relevance in light of the "specific point" she is making.

> The role of ideology—and the particular ideology you allude to—is captured in the discussions of alternate schemas that are enacted. I don't go into the issue of signification or any of the other modalities specifically as I did not see how it would help to make the specific point I am trying to make here.

Thus, in combination, both sets of responses establish boundaries around what Martha was willing to revise and helped sustain her vision for the paper.

A final illustration is offered in Ann Cunliffe's experience of re-writing "Social Poetics as Management Inquiry: A Dialogical Approach." Reviewers were concerned that her situation of social poetics was "largely at the surface of existing work in conversational analysis and other analytic branches" and suggested that a re-writing of the paper should be much better grounded in the literature on ethnomethodology, storytelling, narratives, and metaphor. While she acknowledged that social poetics needed to be better located theoretically, she disagreed with the literatures they had specified because they incorporated different ontological and epistemological assumptions. Indeed, she wrote that disagreement into the text of the final article underscoring it with the phrase, "what makes social poetics so different from these other methods . . ."

REFLECTIONS ON THE RE-WRITTEN MANUSCRIPTS

In the preceding sections in this chapter, we have highlighted the social dimension of writing journal articles as manuscripts are engaged and responded to by members of the larger research community. Through their reactions, challenges and suggestions, colleagues, reviewers and editors participate in the re-writing of the manuscript. In particular, they act in their comments to focus, render more cogent and occasionally suggest new theorized storylines that they believe will provide the most significant information for journal audiences. This level of engagement is sometimes surprising to authors. For example, the level of involvement by reviewers in the paper by Karen Golden-Biddle and Huggy Rao caused Huggy to comment one day that, in qualitative research, the reviewers in effect become "coauthors." Taking this comment a little farther, David Boje remarked at the end of the interview, "I don't think it's my paper anymore. It is group writing. I'm just one of the players."

All the authors indicated that their manuscripts had been considerably strengthened through this engagement and were proud of the papers emerging from it. At the same time, a number of them also reflected on what they had given up as the manuscripts were iteratively re-written in light of the disciplinary community's responses. For example, in the increased emphasis given in the review process to theorizing the storyline, Janet Dukerich noted that, even though the "Eye on the Mirror" is her "most favorite paper," she feels that the story of the Port Authority started "to become sterile" as less and less of the field story remained through revisions. Similarly, Bob Gephart expressed regret over refocusing his paper on methods as opposed to a theorized storyline regarding the myth of organization. He indicated that he felt a responsibility to the widows and family members of the men who died to tell the story that the idea of organization itself is a myth.

Considering the increased paper space devoted to explaining and justifying her inductive methods, Wanda Orlikowski considered that,

> What was lost is a clarity of purpose. The paper feels like it is trying to do multiple things—so, on the one hand it is a story about CASE tools and

organizational change, and issues associated with implementation and use, but on the other hand it also reads like a justification for interpretive research in the Information Systems field. It feels like the paper has a split identity, a condition brought on by the review process. Perhaps it is what was needed at the time. Perhaps it was obligatory then given the state of the field for the paper to explain and be explicit about the method. If the paper feels a little unsatisfactory in the reading of it today, then at the time it may have helped the acceptance of qualitative research methods in the Information Systems field.

While Mike Pratt offered that "overall, this has been one of the more positive experiences," he also pointed to some of the core ideas that he hated to give up (all the while recognizing that they had to go). He commented:

To be frank, I like the "Identity Menu" frame . . . while I understand the deficits of that metaphor I still like it. And I still have people talk to me about identity menus. . . people have multiple [identities.] Organizations have multiple [identities] . . . [and there are] multiple organizational identities interfacing with multiple individual identities—my gut says its true, but data didn't speak to it. The problem is socialization is messier than how it is depicted. I think still there is some messiness that gets cleaned out when you write. That said, nothing was dropped that I thought should not have been dropped.

Geoff Walsham depicted the final version of his article with Sundeep Sahay as "a testament to the fact that the reviewing process can improve manuscripts." He offered that the "the reviewers were very helpful on this manuscript," and that the "final version of this paper is a considerable improvement over the original submission." Nevertheless, in reflecting on the "limitations of a paper-length article," he noted it "is a shame in a way" that although the first version had incorporated both actor network and structuration theories to "inform the field work," for the final version, they deleted structuration theory because the reviewers indicated they couldn't have "two theories in one paper because not enough space was devoted to either."

Finally, as Ann Cunliffe came to understand just how "substantial" her revision of her submitted manuscript would be—that it would, in effect, result in her crafting a new manuscript whose theorized storyline would focus on language as ontology as opposed to an account of how we incorporate the discourse of everyday living into management theory—she realized that the ideas in the initial draft paper, in fact, did not have to die. She did find another publication outlet for it. As she explained,

You reach a point where you say, "is it worth revising," and that first letter the editor sent me had that word "substantial," but the reviewer comments were so helpful and some of the things I was reading made me feel it was worth doing that substantial revision. But I also felt the original paper had merit.

CONCLUSION

Although we often assume that the publication version of a manuscript is close to what was originally submitted (perhaps wishing to believe this is the normal case!), the manuscript journeys portrayed in this chapter show re-writing as a significant and essential feature of the community review process. Writing and re-writing our manuscripts along their journeys takes time as we collectively work toward the crafting of a coherent and compelling theorized storyline that brings the field and academic worlds together and makes a disciplinary contribution. Indeed, it is quite an intensive as well as extensive community endeavor, as the manuscript is circulated among colleagues for their comments and importantly, their reception. Getting a rare glimpse into authors' experiences of this review process portrayed in this chapter helps us gain access to what it takes to navigate this collectively bounded creation of disciplinary knowledge.

Above all, the manuscript journeys convey the importance of being willing as individual authors to involve the community in our work early and often as we develop our field stories, select theoretical locations and craft theorized storylines. In particular, the authors' experiences show that such involvement is both formal and informal. Hallway conversations as well as seminars can source and clarify ideas. Moreover, we discerned how bringing others in is only partially about getting positive suggestions into the developing manuscript. It is also importantly about noticing readers' various receptions to the manuscript and processing their challenging feedback. What resonates with readers? What intrigues them? What do they understand the manuscript to be saying? What challenging issues do they raise? What literatures do they suggest?

The journeys also point to an active, not passive, community involvement. When we allow community members to participate in the development of our manuscript, we are permitting their responses to inform our re-examination of the developing manuscript. Whether or not particular comments and suggestions are ultimately incorporated or rendered significant in the developing manuscript, there is a necessary reexamination, or reconsideration of elements such as the basis structure of the theorized storyline, the relationship between the informing field story and its theoretical location, the representation of the field story, and so on. Thus, through community involvement, we are necessarily engaging with readers to help us see and realize what is not clear about our own work, to actively consider our work in different terms and from different perspectives.

Finally, the journeys highlight that vis-à-vis community involvement, it is important that we, as authors, recognize and sustain the necessary tension between the story envisioned by the community and the story we want to tell from our field experiences and our particular philosophical and epistemological commitments. Although the authors profiled in this chapter acknowledged and dealt thoughtfully with the challenges posed by reviewer comments, they also and importantly preserved the tension by not doing everything the reviewers suggested. Rather than regarding comments as dictates for revision, instead authors took them as guides and challenges to gain perspective on their manuscript. Thus, in re-writing the manuscript, we need to actively consider community comments while retaining a sense of the story we want to tell.

CONCLUDING COMMENTS

W e wrote both editions of this book to encourage discussions of writing and, more generally, to demystify the process of writing for journal articles. What is involved in such writing? What are the demands of producing this particular genre writing? What does writing as a social process look like in our disciplinary communities? By placing writing matters center stage, we hope that we have provided you, our readers, with thought-provoking and practical avenues for addressing such questions and becoming more knowledgeable about writing. Through dialogue on writing, we believe that we further strengthen our qualitative investigative efforts, we more fully articulate and integrate our field stories with the ideas and concerns of the disciplinary communities in which we work, and we more self-consciously shape the texts we write.

In writing this new edition, we intentionally sought to open up and explore the space between traditional dichotomies that shape our writing, such as theory and data. We reframed these dichotomies in order to discern and more creatively negotiate central issues authors face in composing qualitative research. These issues include: writing together our field and academic worlds in theorized storylines; conveying the institutional and human aspects of our character as storytellers; and in tracing the processes involved in the journals of manuscripts through their early origins to publication, deciding whether to incorporate or leave behind reviewer comments. In this edition, we portray the various ways authors negotiated these issues, providing options rather than "algorithms" (Gephart, 2004) for readers to consider in their own writing efforts.

We took this approach because we believe that we have too much to lose if we don't become knowledgeable of and conscious about how we write. Significantly, we lose the ability to express the multivocality of our data. We also lose the ability to portray complications in action and the possibilities for action that existed for the people we studied at the time we studied them. In our quest to render decisive contributions to the literature, we develop overly certain theoretical explanations. Ultimately, then, by remaining ignorant of writing matters, we severely limit the possibilities for converting our field engagement with people's conversations and lives into theoretically relevant insights and claims.

At the point of bringing this book to a close, we continue to appreciate the complexity of the task we are setting out to accomplish when we sit down to write at our keyboards or with our pencil and paper. We are also continuing to learn new ways of strengthening writing efforts and navigating the space between traditional dichotomies that emerge in writing. In our first chapter, we played off the "just write it up" injunction to outline this complexity in writing. By doing this, we highlighted a misperception of writing as the residual task in our research efforts. Certainly, writing is not residual! Mary Jo Hatch put it very well when she reflected that perhaps we should draw our boundaries around the research process more widely. Instead of assuming that an investigative effort has achieved closure when the analysis is complete and insights have been formulated, we should extend our definition of research to include the drafting of a formal paper, revision efforts during the review process and the readings the work receives from our community of scientists. Indeed, as our discussion of manuscripts' journeys to submission in Chapter 5 indicated, analysis and rework grew out of and continued through the review process.

From this vantage point, writing is one of several research processes in which we need to develop increasing competency. While each of us needs to cultivate a personal process for writing, there is also much to gain from articulating community wisdom on writing. It is in this spirit that we offer some practices we hope are useful in considering matters of writing and in strengthening our personal and community writing processes.

WRITING AND RE-WRITING

Experienced writers testify that good writing demands investments of time and effort in a recursive writing process (Dillard, 1989; Elbow, 1981; Fulwiler, 1987; Lamott, 1995). Certainly, the stories and storylines that our data-gathering efforts authorize us to write precede the main writing stage of our work. Yet, in a very real sense, they also grow out of the writing process (Richardson,

1994). By generating theoretically relevant insights, and writing them out on paper, we are able to work out how the field world and the ideas of our disciplinary community interact and to make them available for our and our colleagues' examination. Writing them out, we and others can see what works, what needs development, what is problematic, what may be more or less interesting. Yet, early on in our writing endeavors, we don't realize the central role of re-writing our texts to make a contribution to the literatures of our disciplinary communities. As we depicted in Chapter 5, when we and others interact with our words, we inevitably modify and re-write what we are trying to say. We have to iteratively re-write our way to writing that displays orderliness, coherence, and a conscious strategy for theorizing our experiences in the field. Knowing this makes us be more patient with each draft. Anne Smith (2002) illuminates this process by portraying the personal sensemaking journey in developing her research for publication. She articulates a useful model of this journey, beginning with data analysis and continuing through publication.

SHARING

We think it is important to share, from the very beginning, both what we write about and our experiences of writing. As we write successive drafts, we need readers to tell us how they experience our words (Elbow, 1981), how they understand the theoretical stories we are trying to tell, and what significance they see for the work. The authors whose manuscripts were profiled in Chapter 5 underscored the importance of getting feedback from colleagues and their willingness to provide it, early and during the process of writing and re-writing our manuscripts. More than one remarked how useful the practice of getting feedback is because others can often discern the potential for contribution in the work. Similarly, sharing experiences of the writing process helps to break the silence, and creates support for this lengthy process. This suggests that we should find ways to make writing a social process from the beginning, creating our own informal network of readers who will agree to respond to each others' writing before it is submitted for review.

READING

Finally, we have found the process of reading manuscripts with an eye toward how they are written to be invaluable. As this book indicates, reading in this manner not only helps to demystify the writing process, but by becoming aware of the variety of writing evident in journal manuscripts, reading also helps us to develop our own writing style and voice. By looking at variations in written presentation and style, we find that we more closely identify with the work of some authors while finding that we perhaps do not want to emulate others (Locke & Brazelton, 1997). This helps us to identify over time what we want to sound like on paper.

As we close this book, we look forward to continuing conversations about writing matters with you.

REFERENCES

Adler, P. A., & Adler, P. (1988). Intense loyalty in organizations: A case study of college athletics. *Administrative Science Quarterly, 33,* 401–417.

Ailon-Souday, G., & Kunda, G. (2003). The local selves of global workers: The social construction of national identity in the face of organizational globalization. *Organization Studies, 24,* 1073–1096.

Arndt M., & Bigelow, B. (2000). Presenting structural innovation in an institutional environment: Hospitals' use of impression management. *Administrative Science Quarterly, 45,* 494–522.

Aronson, N. (1984). Science as a claims making activity: Implications for social problems research. In J. W. Schneider & J. Kitsuse (Eds.), *Studies in the sociology of social problems* (pp. 1–30). Norwood, NJ: Ablex.

Atkinson, P. (1990). *The ethnographic imagination.* London: Routledge.

Barker, J. R. (1993). Tightening the iron cage: Concertive control in self managing teams. *Administrative Science Quarterly, 38,* 408–437.

Barley, S. R. (1983). Semiotics and the study of occupational and organizational cultures. *Administrative Science Quarterly, 28,* 393–413.

Barley, S. R. (1986). Technology as an occasion for structuring: Evidence from observations of CT scanners and the social order of radiology departments. *Administrative Science Quarterly, 31,* 78–108.

Bazerman, C. (1988). *Shaping written knowledge: The genre and activity of the experimental article in science.* Madison: University of Wisconsin Press.

Bazerman, C. (1993). Intertextual self-fashioning: Gould and Lewontin's representations of the literature. In J. Selzer (Ed.), *Understanding scientific prose* (pp. 20–41). Madison: University of Wisconsin Press.

Bazerman, C. (1996). Editor's introduction. In D. Winsor (Ed.), *Writing like an engineer* (pp. vii–viii). Mahwah, NJ: Lawrence Erlbaum.

Bazerman, C., & Paradis, J. (1991). *Textual dynamics of the professions: Historical and contemporary studies of writing in professional communities.* Madison: University of Wisconsin Press.

Bazerman, C., & Prior, P. (2004). *What writing does and how it does it: An introduction to analyzing texts and textual practices.* Mahwah, NJ: Lawrence Erlbaum.

Bechky, B. A. (2003). Sharing meaning across occupational communities: The transformation of understanding on a production floor. *Organization Science, 14,* 312–330.

Becker, H. (1986). *Writing for social scientists.* Chicago: University of Chicago Press.

Beyer, J. M., Chanove, R. G., & Fox, W. B. (1995). The review process and the fates of manuscripts submitted to AMJ. *Academy of Management Journal, 38,* 1219–1260.

Biggart, N. W., & Hamilton, G. G. (1984). The power of obedience. *Administrative Science Quarterly, 29,* 540–549.

Billig, M. (1993). Psychology, rhetoric, and cognition. In R. H. Roberts & J. M. Good (Eds.), *The recovery of rhetoric: Persuasive discourse and disciplinarity in the human sciences* (pp. 119–136). Charlottesville: University Press of Virginia.

Bills, D. B. (1987). Costs, commitment, and rewards: Factors influencing the design and implementation of internal labor markets. *Administrative Science Quarterly, 32,* 202–221.

Bochner, A. (2001). Narrative's virtues. *Qualitative Inquiry, 7*(2), 131–157.

Bochner, A. P., & Ellis, C. (1996). Introduction: Talking over ethnography. In C. Ellis & A. Bochner (Eds.), *Composing ethnography: Alternative forms of qualitative writing* (pp. 13–45). Lanham, MD: AltaMira.

Boice, R. (2000). *Advice for new faculty members: Nihil nimus.* Boston: Allyn & Bacon.

Boje, D. M. (1991). The storytelling organization: A study of story performance in an office-supply firm. *Administrative Science Quarterly, 36,* 106–126.

Boje, D. M. (1995). Stories of the storytelling organization. *Academy of Management Journal, 38,* 997–1035.

Booth, W. C. (1961). *The rhetoric of fiction.* Chicago: University of Chicago Press.

Booth, W. C. (1967). The revival of rhetorics. In M. Steinmann, Jr. (Ed.), *New rhetorics* (pp. 1–15). New York: Scribner's.

Brooks, C., & Warren, R. P. (1938). *Understanding poetry.* New York: Holt, Rinehart and Winston.

Brooks, I. (2003). Systemic exchange: Responsibility for angst. *Organization Studies, 24,* 125–141.

Bruner, J. (1996). *The culture of education.* Cambridge, MA: Harvard University Press.

Burke, K. (1950). *A rhetoric of motives.* Berkeley: University of California Press.

Calas, M., & Smircich, L. (1991). Voicing seduction to silence leadership. *Organization Studies, 12,* 567–602.

Campbell, D. T. (1975). Degrees of freedom and the case study. *Comparative Political Studies, I*(8), 178–193.

Charmaz, K. (1999). Stories of suffering: Subjective tales and research narratives. *Qualitative Health Research, 9,* 362–382.

Cheek, J., & Ballantyne, A. (2001). Moving them on and in: The process of searching for and selecting an aged care facility. *Qualitative Health Research, 11,* 221–237.

Cheek, J., & Gibson, T. (2003). Issues impacting on registered nursing providing care to older people in acute care setting. *NT Research, 8,* 134–149.

Clifford, J. (1983). On ethnographic authority. *Representations, 1,* 118–146.

Clifford, J., & Marcus, G. E. (1986). *Writing culture: The poetics and politics of ethnography.* Berkeley: University of California Press.

Corley, K. G., & Gioia, D. A. (2004). Identity ambiguity and change in the wake of a corporate spin-off. *Administrative Science Quarterly, 49,* 173–208.

Coupland, C., & Brown, A. D. (2004). Constructing organizational identities on the Web: A case study of Royal Dutch Shell. *Journal of Management Studies, 41,* 1325–1348.

Cozzens, S. (1985). Comparing the sciences: Citation context analysis of papers from neuropharmacology and the sociology of science. *Social Studies of Science, 15,* 127–153.

Cunliffe, A. (2002). Social poetics as management inquiry: A dialogical approach. *Journal of Management Inquiry, 11,* 128–146.

Czarniawska, B. (1986). The management of meaning in the Polish crisis. *Journal of Management Studies, 23*(3), 313–329.

Czarniawska, B. (1999). *Writing management: Organization theory as a literary genre.* New York: Oxford University Press.

Czarniawska, B. (2004). *Narratives in social science research.* Thousand Oaks, CA: Sage.

Denis, J.-L., Langley, A., & Pineault, M. (2000). Becoming a leader in a complex organization. *Journal of Management Studies, 37,* 1063–1099.

Denzin, N. (1994). The art and politics of interpretation. In N. K. Denzin & Y. S. Lincoln (Eds.), *Handbook of qualitative research.* Thousand Oaks, CA: Sage.

Dillard, A. (1989). *The writing life.* New York: HarperPerennial.

Dutton, J. E., & Dukerich, J. M. (1991). Keeping an eye on the mirror: Image and identity in organizational adaptation. *Academy of Management Journal, 34,* 517–554.

Dutton, J. E., Worline, M., Frost, P. J., & Lilius, J. (2006, March). Explaining compassion organizing. *Administrative Science Quarterly.*

Edmondson, A. (2002). The local and variegated nature of learning in organizations: A group-level perspective. *Organization Science, 13,* 128–146.

Edmonson, R. (1984). *Rhetoric in sociology.* London: Macmillan.

Eisenhardt, K. M. (1989). Making fast strategic decisions in high-velocity environments. *Academy of Management Journal, 32,* 543–576.

Elbow, P. (1981). *Writing with power: Techniques for mastering the writing process.* New York: Oxford University Press.

Ellis, C., & Bochner, A. P. (1996). *Composing ethnography: Alternative forms of qualitative writing.* Lanham, MD: AltaMira.

Elsbach, K. D., & Bhattacharya, C. B. (2001). Defining who you are by what you're not: Organizational disidentification and the National Rifle Association. *Organization Science, 12,* 393–413.

Elsbach, K. D., & Kramer, R. J. (2003). Assessing creativity in Hollywood pitch meetings: Evidence for a dual-process model of creativity judgments. *Academy of Management Journal, 46,* 283–301.

Feldman, M. (1995). *Strategies for interpreting qualitative data.* Thousand Oaks, CA: Sage.

Feldman, M. (2004). Resources in emerging structures and processes of change. *Organization Science, 15,* 295–309.

Fine, G. A. (1988, Summer). The ten commandments of writing. *American Sociologist,* pp. 152–157.

Franklin, J. (1994). *Writing for story.* New York: Penguin.

Frost, P. J., & Taylor, R. N. (1995). Partisan perspective: A multiple-level interpretation of the manuscript review process in social science journals. In L. L. Cummings & P. J. Frost (Eds.), *Publishing in the organizational sciences* (pp. 4–43). Thousand Oaks, CA: Sage.

Fulweiler, T. (1987). *Teaching with writing.* Upper Montclair, NJ: Boynton/Cook.

Geertz, C. (1973). *The interpretation of cultures.* New York: Basic Books.

Geertz, C. (1983). Blurred genres: The refiguration of social thought. In *Local knowledge: Further essays in interpretive anthropology* (pp. 19–35). New York: Basic Books.

Geertz, C. (1988). *Works and lives: The anthropologist as author.* Palo Alto, CA: Stanford University Press.

Gephart, R. P. (1984). Making sense of organizationally based environmental disasters. *Journal of Management, 10,* 205–225.

Gephart, R. P. (1986). Deconstructing the defense for quantification in social science: A content analysis of journal articles on the parametric strategy. *Qualitative Sociology, 9,* 126–144.

Gephart, R. P. (1988). *Ethnostatistics: Qualitative foundations for quantitative research.* Newbury Park, CA: Sage.

Gephart, R. P. (1993). The textual approach: Risk and blame in disaster sensemaking. *Academy of Management Journal, 36,* 1465–1514.

Gephart, R. P. (2004). Qualitative research and the *Academy of Management Journal. Academy of Management Journal, 47,* 454–462.

Gersick, C. J. G., Bartunek, J. M., & Dutton, J. E. (2000). Learning from academia: The importance of relationships in professional life. *Academy of Management Journal, 43,* 1026–1027.

Gersick, C. J. G. (1988). Time and transition in work teams: Toward a new model of group development. *Academy of Management Journal, 31,* 9–41.

Gersick, C. J. G. (1994). Pacing strategic change: The case of a new venture. *Academy of Management Journal, 37,* 9–45.

Gilbert, N. (1976). The transformation of research findings into scientific knowledge. *Social Studies of Science, 6,* 281–306.

Gilbert, N. (1977. Referencing as persuasion. *Social Studies of Science, 7,* 113–122.

Glaser, B., & Strauss, A. (1967). *The discovery of grounded theory.* Chicago: Aldine.

Golden, K. A. (1992). The individual and organizational culture: Strategies for action in highly-ordered contexts. *Journal of Management Studies, 2,* 1–22.

Golden-Biddle, K., & Locke, K. (1993). Appealing work: An investigation of how ethnographic texts convince. *Organization Science, 4,* 595–616.

Golden-Biddle, K., & Rao, H. V. (1997). Breaches in the board room: Organizational identity and conflicts of commitment in a non-profit organization. *Organization Science, 8,* 593–611.

Golden-Biddle, K., Locke, K., & Reay, T. (2006). Using knowledge in management studies. *Journal of Management Inquiry, 15*(3).

Gopal, A., & Prasad, P. (2000). Understanding GDSS in symbolic context: Shifting the focus from technology to interaction. *MIS Quarterly, 24,* 509–546.

Gould, S. J., & Lewontin, R. (1979). The spandrels of San Marco and the Panglossian paradigm: A critique of the adaptationist programme. Proceedings of the Royal Society of London. *Biological Sciences, 205,* 581–598.

Gubrium, J., & Holstein, J. (1997). *The new language of qualitative method.* New York: Oxford University Press.

Gusfield, J. (1981). *The culture of public problems: Drinking, driving and symbolic order.* Chicago: University of Chicago Press.

Hamilton, E., & Cairns, H. (1961). *Plato: The collected dialogues.* Princeton, NJ: Princeton University Press.

Hirschhorn, L., & Gilmore, T. (1980). The application of family therapy concepts to influencing organizational behavior. *Administrative Science Quarterly, 25,* 18–37.

Holm, P. (1995). The dynamics of institutionalization: Transformation processes in Norwegian fisheries. *Administrative Science Quarterly, 40,* 398–422.

Howard-Grenville, J. A. (2005). The persistence of flexible organizational routines: The role of agency and organizational context. *Organization Science, 16,* 618–636.

Huff, S. A. (1998). *Writing for scholarly publication.* Thousand Oaks, CA: Sage.

Hunter, A. (1990). Rhetoric in research: Networks of knowledge. In A. Hunter (Ed.), *The rhetoric of social research: Understood and believed* (pp. 1–22). New Brunswick, NJ: Rutgers University Press.

Ibarra, H. (1999). Provisional selves: Experimenting with image and identity in professional adaptation. *Administrative Science Quarterly, 44,* 764–791.

Isabella, L. A. (1990). Evolving interpretations as a change unfolds: How managers construe key organizational events. *Academy of Management Journal, 33,* 7–41.

Iser, W. (1978). *The act of reading: A theory of aesthetic response.* Baltimore, MD: Johns Hopkins University Press.

Iser, W. (1989). *Prospecting: From reader response to literary anthropology.* Baltimore, MD: Johns Hopkins University Press.

Kahn, W. A. (1993). Caring for the caregivers: Patterns of organizational caregiving. *Administrative Science Quarterly, 38,* 539–563.

Kilduff, M. (1993). Deconstructing organizations. *Academy of Management Review, 18,* 13–31.

Knorr-Cetina, K. (1981). *The manufacture of knowledge: An essay on the constructivist and contextual nature of science.* Elmsford, NY: Pergamon.

Kram, K. E. (1983). Phases of the mentor relationship. *Academy of Management Journal, 26,* 608–625.

Kram, K. E., & Isabella, L. A. (1985). Mentoring alternatives: The role of peer relationships in career development. *Academy of Management Journal, 28,* 110–132.

Lammers, C. J. (1988). The interorganizational control of an occupied country. *Administrative Science Quarterly, 33,* 438–457.

Lamott, A. (1995). *Bird by bird. Some instructions on writing and life.* Garden City, NY: Anchor Books.

Langer, S. (1964). *Philosophy in a new key: A study in the symbolism of reason, rite, and art.* New York: Mentor Books.

Langton, J. (1984). The ecological theory of bureaucracy: The case of Josiah Wedgwood and the British pottery industry. *Administrative Science Quarterly, 29,* 330–354.

Latour, B. (1987). *Science in action: How to follow scientists and engineers through society.* Cambridge, MA: Harvard University Press.

Latour, B., & Woolgar, S. (1986). *Laboratory life: The construction of scientific facts.* Princeton, NJ: Princeton University Press.

Law, J., & Williams, R. (1982). Putting the facts together: A study of scientific persuasion. *Social Studies of Science, 12,* 535–558.

Llewellyn, S. (2001). "Two way" windows: Clinicians as medical managers. *Organization Studies, 22,* 593–602.

Locke, K. (1996). Who's re-writing grounded theory over 25 years later? *Journal of Management Inquiry, 5,* 239–245.

Locke, K. (2001). *Grounded theory in management research.* London: Sage.

Locke, K., & Brazelton, J. (1997). Why do we ask them to write? Or, whose writing is it, anyway? *Journal of Management Education, 21,* 24–43.

Locke, K., & Golden-Biddle, K. (1997). Constructing opportunities for contribution: Intertextual coherence and problematization in organizational studies. *Academy of Management Journal, 40,* 1023–1062.

Locke, K., Golden-Biddle, K., & Feldman, M. (2004). Imaginative theorizing. In D. H. Nagao (Ed.), *Best paper proceedings of the 64th Annual Meeting of the Academy of Management,* New Orleans, Louisiana.

Locke, K. D. (1996). A funny thing happened: The management of consumer emotions in service encounters. *Organization Science, 7,* 40–59.

Lyne, J. (1993). Angels in the architecture: A Burkean inventional perspective on "Spandrels." In J. Selzer (Ed.), *Understanding scientific prose* (pp. 144–158). Madison: University of Wisconsin Press.

Maitlis, S. (2004). Taking it from the top: How CEOs influence (and fail to influence) their boards. *Organization Studies, 25,* 1275–1311.

March, J., & Simon, H. (1958). *Organizations.* New York: John Wiley.

Marcus, G. (1980). Rhetoric and the ethnographic genre in anthropological research. *Current Anthropology, 21,* 507–510.

Marcus, G., & Cushman, D. (1982). Ethnographies as texts. *Annual Review of Anthropology, 11,* 25–69.

Marcus, G., & Fischer, M. (1986). *Anthropology as cultural critique.* Chicago: University of Chicago Press.

Markus, L. M., Majchrzak, A., & Gasser, L. (2002). A design theory for systems that support emergent knowledge processes. *MIS Quarterly, 26,* 179–212.

Martin, J. (1990). Deconstructing organizational taboos: The suppression of gender conflict in organizations. *Organization Science, 1*(4), 339–359.

Martin, J., Knopoff, K., & Beckman, C. (1998). An alternative to bureaucratic impersonality and emotional labor: Bounded emotionality at the Body Shop. *Administrative Science Quarterly, 43,* 429–469.

McCloskey, D. N. (1985). *The rhetoric of economics.* Madison: University of Wisconsin Press.

McCloskey, D. N. (1990). *If you're so smart: The narrative of economic expertise.* Chicago: University of Chicago Press.

McCloskey, D. N. (1994). *Knowledge and persuasion in economics.* Cambridge, UK: Cambridge University Press.

McKinley, W., Mone, M. A., & Moon, G. (1999). Determinants and development of schools in organization theory. *Academy of Management Review, 28,* 634–648.

Miller, W. L., Crabtree, B. F., McDaniel, R., & Stange, K. C. (1998). Understanding change in primary care practice using complexity theory. *Journal of Family Practice, 46,* 369–377.

Miner, A. S., Bassoff, P., & Moorman, C. (2001). Organizational improvisation and learning: A field study. *Administrative Science Quarterly, 46,* 304–337.

Mone, M., & McKinley, W. (1993). The uniqueness value and its consequences for organization studies. *Journal of Management Inquiry, 2,* 284–296.

Morner, K., & Rausch, R. (1991). *NTC's dictionary of literary terms.* Chicago: NTC Publishing.

Morse, J. M., & Pooler, C. (2002). Patient-family-nurse interactions in the trauma resuscitation room. *American Journal of Critical Care, 11,* 240–249.

Mottier, V. (2005). The interpretive turn: History, memory, and storage in qualitative research. *Forum Qualitative Sozialforschung/Forum: Qualitative Social Research, 6*(2), Art. 33.

Mulkay, M. (1995). *The word and the world: Explorations in the form of sociological analysis.* Boston: Allen & Unwin.

Mumby, D., & Putnam, L. (1992). Bounded rationality and organizing: A feminist critique. *Academy of Management Review, 17,* 465–486.

Nelson, K., Nadkarni, S., Narayanan, V., & Ghods, M. (2000). Understanding software operations support expertise: A revealed causal mapping approach. *MIS Quarterly, 24*(3), 475–507.

Ng, W., & DeCock, C. (2002). Battle in the boardroom: A discursive perspective. *Journal of Management Studies, 39,* 23–49.

Ofori-Dankwa, J., & Julian, S. D. (2005). From thought to theory to school: The role of contextual factors in the evolution of schools of management thought. *Organization Studies, 26,* 1307–1329.

Orlikowski, W. J. (1993, September). CASE tools as organizational change: Investigating incremental and radical changes in systems development. *MIS Quarterly,* pp. 309–340.

Orlikowski, W. J. (2002). Knowing in practice: Enacting a collective capability in distributed organizing. *Organization Science, 13,* 249–273.

Patton, M. Q. (2002). *Qualitative research and evaluation methods* (3rd ed.). Thousand Oaks, CA: Sage.

Pentland, B. T. (1992). Organizing moves in software support hotlines. *Administrative Science Quarterly, 37,* 527–548.

Perlow, L. A. (1999). The time famine: Toward a sociology of work time. *Administrative Science Quarterly, 44,* 57–81.

Perlow, L. A., Okhuysen, G. A., & Repenning, N. P. (2002). The speed trap: Exploring the relationship between decision making and temporal context. *Academy of Management Journal, 45,* 931–955.

Pinder, C., & Bourgeois, V. W. (1982). Controlling tropes in administrative science. *Administrative Science Quarterly, 27,* 641–652.

Pratt, M. G, Rockmann, K., & Kaufmann, J. (2006). Constructing professional identity: The role of work and identity learning cycles in the customization of identity among medical residents. *Academy of Management Journal, 49,* 235–262.

Rabinow, P., & Sullivan, W. M. (1987). The interpretive turn: A second look. In P. Rabinow & W. M. Sullivan (Eds.), *Interpretive social science* (pp. 1–30). Berkeley: University of California Press.

Ranft, A. L., & Lord, M. D. (2002). Acquiring new technologies and capabilities: A grounded model of acquisition implementation. *Organization Science, 13,* 420–441.

Rankin, E. (2001). *The work of writing: Insights and strategies for academics and professionals.* New York: John Wiley.

Reay, T., Golden-Biddle, K., & GermAnn, K. (2006). Legitimizing a new role: Small wins and micro-processes of change. *Academy of Management Journal 49*(5).

Richardson, L. (1990). *Writing strategies: Reaching diverse audiences.* Thousand Oaks, CA: Sage.

Richardson, L. (1994). Writing: A method of inquiry. In N. K. Denzin & Y. S. Lincoln (Eds.), *Handbook of qualitative research.* Thousand Oaks, CA: Sage.

Riley, P. (1983. A structurationist account of political culture. *Administrative Science Quarterly, 28,* 414–437.

Rorty, R. (1967). *The linguistic turn: Recent essays in philosophical method.* Chicago: University of Chicago Press.

Rorty, R. (1982). *The consequences of pragmatism.* Minneapolis: University of Minnesota Press.

Rorty, R. (1989). *Contingency, irony and solidarity.* New York: Cambridge University Press.

Ross, J., & Staw, B. M. (1993). Organizational escalation and exit: Lessons from the Shoreham nuclear power plant. *Academy of Management Journal, 36,* 701–732.

Rousseau, D. (1995). Publishing from a reviewer's perspective. In L. L. Cummings & P. J. Frost (Eds.), *Publishing in the organizational sciences* (pp. 151–163). Thousand Oaks, CA: Sage.

Sandberg, J. (2000). Understanding human competence at work: An interpretative approach. *Academy of Management Journal, 43,* 9–25.

Sarker, S., & Sahay, S. (2004). Implications of space and time for distributed work: An interpretive study of US-Norwegian systems development teams. *European Journal of Information Systems, 13,* 3–20.

Schultze, U. (2000). A confessional account of an ethnography about knowledge work. *MIS Quarterly, 24,* 3–41.

Selzer, J. (1993). *Understanding scientific prose.* Madison: University of Wisconsin Press.

Shuval, J. T., & Mizrachi, N. (2004). Changing boundaries: Modes of coexistence of alternative and biomedicine. *Qualitative Health Research, 14,* 675–690.

Smith, A. D. (2002). From process data to publication: A personal sensemaking. *Journal of Management Inquiry, 11,* 383–406.

Spector, M., & Kitsuse, J. I. (1977). *Constructing social problems.* Redwood City, CA: Benjamin-Cummings.

Strauss, A. L. (1987). *Qualitative analysis for social scientists.* New York: Cambridge University Press.

Strauss, A. L., & Corbin, J. (1990). *Basics of qualitative research: Grounded theory procedures and techniques.* Newbury Park, CA: Sage.

Sutton, R. I., & Callahan, A. (1987). The stigma of bankruptcy: Spoiled organizational image and its management. *Academy of Management Journal, 30,* 405–436.

Sutton, R. I. (1991). Maintaining norms about expressed emotions: The case of bill collectors. *Administrative Science Quarterly, 36,* 245–268.

Swales, J., & Najjar, H. (1987). The writing of research article introductions. *Written Communication, 4,* 175–191.

Thomas, D. A. (1993). Racial dynamics in cross-race developmental relationships. *Administrative Science Quarterly, 38,* 169–194.

Trauth, E. M., & Jessup, L. M. (2000). Understanding computer-mediated discussions: Positivist and interpretive analyses of group support systems use. *MIS Quarterly, 24,* 43–79.

Turner, B. A. (1976). The organizational and interorganizational development of disasters. *Administrative Science Quarterly, 21,* 378–397.

Turner, P. K. (2004). Mainstreaming alternative medicine: Doing midwifery at the intersection. *Qualitative Health Research, 14,* 644–662.

Van Maanen, J. (1988). *Tales of the field: On writing ethnography.* Chicago: University of Chicago Press.

Van Maanen, J. (1995). *Representation in ethnography*. Thousand Oaks, CA: Sage.

Van Maanen, J., & Schein, E. (1979). Toward a theory of organizational socialization. In B. M. Staw & L. L. Cummings (Eds.), *Research in Organizational Behavior, 1*, 209–264.

Vaughan, D. (1990). Autonomy, interdependence, and social control: NASA and the space shuttle *Challenger. Administrative Science Quarterly, 35*, 225–257.

Walsham, G., & Sahay, S. (1999). GIS for district-level administration in India: Problems and opportunities. *MIS Quarterly, 23*, 39–66.

Watson, T. J. (1995). Shaping the story: Rhetoric, persuasion, and creative writing in organizational ethnography. *Studies in Cultures, Organizations and Societies, 1*, 301–311.

Weick, K. E. (1988). Enacted environments in crisis situations. *Journal of Management Studies, 25*, 305–317.

Weick, K. E. (1993). The collapse of sensemaking in organizations: The Mann Gulch disaster. *Administrative Science Quarterly, 38*, 628–652.

Weick, K. E. (1995). Editing innovation into *Administrative Science Quarterly*. In L. L. Cummings & P. J. Frost (Eds.), *Publishing in the organizational sciences*. Thousand Oaks, CA: Sage.

Whiteman, G., & Cooper, W. H. (2000). Ecological embeddedness. *Academy of Management Journal, 43*, 1265–1282.

Winsor, D. (1993). Constructing scientific knowledge in Gould and Lewontin's "The spandrels of San Marco." In J. Selzer (Ed.), *Understanding scientific prose* (pp. 127–143). Madison: University of Wisconsin Press.

Winsor, D. (1996). *Writing like an engineer: A rhetorical education*. Mahwah, NJ: Lawrence Erlbaum.

Wolcott, H. (1990). *Writing up qualitative research*. Newbury Park, CA: Sage.

Wolcott, H. (2001). *Writing up qualitative research* (2nd ed.). Thousand Oaks, CA: Sage.

Yan, A., & Gray, B. (1994). Bargaining power: Management control and performance in United States–China joint ventures: A comparative case study. *Academy of Management Journal, 37*, 1478–1717.

INDEX

A-rhetorical view, of scientific
  writing, 19
Abstract, journal, 48
Academic audience, 15
Academic speak, 11
Actor network theory, 84
Adler, P., 78
Ailon Souday, G., 16, 73
Alternative perspective. *See*
  Problematizing the literature
Anthropology, new research
  traditions in, 19
Arndt, M., 83 (tab), 84, 91–92, 101–102
Aronson, N., 18
Atkinson, P., 19
Atypical storyteller, 75
Audience, for professional writing,
  11–12, 14–17, 18, 62

Ballantyne, A., 16
Bankruptcy, 22
Barker, J. R., 48–49, 55–56
Barley, S. R., 16, 34
Bartunek, J. M., 20
Bassoff, P., 38
Bazerman, C., 3, 9, 20, 26, 33
Bechky, B. A., 35, 42, 52
Becker, H., 2, 4, 16
Beckraan, C., 30
Beyer, J. M., 86
Bhattacharya, C. B., 21
Bigelow, B., 83 (tab), 84, 91, 101–102
Biggart, N. W., 21
Billig, M., 19

Bills, D. B., 37
Board functioning, 35, 40–41, 49–51
Bochner, A. P., 3, 14
Boice, R., 1
Boilerplate justification, 8, 76
Boje, D. M., 42, 82 (tab), 87,
  88, 92, 108
Booth, W. C., 3, 14, 52–53, 62
Bourgeois, V. W., 11, 19
Brazelton, J., 116
"Breaches in the Boardroom:
  Organizational Identity and
  Conflict of Commitment in a
  Non-Profit Organization"
  (Golden-Biddle & Rao), 90–91
Brooks, C., 10
Brooks, I., 65
Brown, A. D., 16
Bruner, J., 1, 3, 64
Burke, K., 14

Cairns, H., 61
Calas, M., 19
Callahan, A., 34
Campbell, D. T., 90
"CASE Tools as Organizational
  Change: Investigating Incremental
  and Radical Changes in Systems
  Development" (Orlikowski), 84
Chanove, R. G., 86
Characterization metaphor, 22
Charmaz, K., 16, 71
Cheek, J., 16, 35, 47
Citations, 34–36

Clifford, J., 1, 19
Colloquialism, 78
Complication, introducing, 57–60
Consensus, researcher, 18, 34
Constructed reality, 14
Continuing controversy assessment
    of literature, 36–37
Contradictory assessment of
    literature, 36–37
Conversation metaphor, 16–17
Cooper, W. H., 77
Corbin, J., 64
Corley, K. G., 28
Coupland, C., 16
Cozzens, S., 18
Crabtree, B. R., 16, 28–29
Cunliffe, A., 83 (tab), 86,
    107–108, 109–110
Cushman, D., 19
Czarniawska, B., 3, 13, 14, 19, 68

Data
    formatting, 69
    multivocal nature of, 26,
        89–90, 113–114
    objectivity and, 70–71
    strength of, 70
    verbatim, 56–57, 69
    weighting, 70
Data-coupling theory, 55–57
Decision making, 16, 43–44, 50
DeCock, C., 35, 50
Denis, J. L., 29
Denzin, N., 76
Dillard, A., 12, 114
Discourse, interesting/persuasive, 17–20
Discrepant references, 33–34
Dissensus within literature, 36–37
Diverse literatures, connecting, 33–34
Dramatic moments, portraying, 22–23
Dukerich, J. M., 55, 82 (tab), 87,
    89, 92, 105, 108
Dutton, J. E., 20, 29, 55, 82 (tab),
    87, 89, 92, 105

Economics, new research traditions in, 19
Editors. See Review process

Edmondson, A., 31, 74
Edmonson, R., 19, 45, 59, 74
Eisenhardt, K. M., 43–44
Elbow, P., 12, 114, 115
Ellis, C., 3, 14
Elsbach, K. D., 21, 41

False rigor, 70
Feldman, M., 4, 10, 83 (tab),
    85–86, 98–99, 105–107
Field-based story, 87–91
    relation to theorized story, 57–60
    rewriting, 87–91
    transporting reader into field, 48
Figurative language, 19
Fine, G. A., 2–3, 48
First person, 11, 66–67, 74–75
Fischer, M., 19
Font size, 69
Football game metaphor, 21
Forms/formats, established, 15
Fox, W. B., 86
Franklin, J., 25, 57
Frost, P. J., 9, 29
Fulweiler, T., 114
"A Funny Thing Happened: The
    Management of Consumer
    Emotions in Service Encounters"
    (Locke), 90

Gasser, L., 16
Geertz, C., 1, 3, 19, 63, 64, 79
Gephart, R. P., 3, 11, 37, 44, 47, 48–49,
    56–57, 82 (tab), 90, 100, 108, 113
GermAnn, K., 15–16, 52
Gersick, C. J. G., 20, 21, 37, 54
Ghods, M., 73
Gibson, T., 16, 35, 47
Gilbert, N., 18, 76
Gilmore, T., 34
Gioia, D. A., 28
"GIS for District-Level Administration in
    India" (Walsham & Sahay), 70–71
Glaser, B., 64, 76
Golden-Biddle, K. A., 10, 14, 15, 16,
    17, 19, 20, 26, 27, 31, 33, 38, 52,
    77, 82 (tab), 90–91, 99, 108

Gopal, A., 39–40
Gould, S. J., 33
Gray, B., 36
Grounded theory, 76, 104
Gubrium, J., 2
Gusfield, J., 14, 18, 79

Hamilton, E., 61
Hamilton, G. G., 21
Hirschhom, L., 34
Holm, P., 37
Holstein, J., 2
Homelessness, 55, 89
Howard-Grenville, J. A., 30–31, 45
Huff, S. A. (1998), 3, 16
Hunter, A., 13, 19

Ibarra, H., 47, 95
Identity, 21, 92, 94–96, 105
Identity customization processes, 95
Implied audience, 62
Implied authorial character, 61–62
Insider language, 15
Interpreting literature, flexibility in, 33
Intertextual coherence
    noncoherence, 36–37
    progressive, 34–36, 40–41, 45–46
    rewriting story for, 96, 99, 100
    synthesized, 33–34, 40
Introductory paragraph, 48–51
Isabella, L. A., 34–35, 38–39
Iser, W., 3, 14

Jessup, L. M., 47
Journal article
    abstract for, 48
    as nonfiction short story, 25
    as proposal of knowledge, 18
    space limitations for, 13–14, 109
Julian, S. D., 15
Juxtaposition, between prior/proposed
    research, 43, 44

Kahn, W. A., 53–55
Kantian perspective on
    writing, 10–11
Kaufmann, J., 47, 83 (tab), 85, 88

"Keeping an Eye on the Mirror:
    Image and Identity in
    Organizational Adaptation"
    (Dutton & Dukerich), 87, 108
Kilduff, M., 19, 33
Kitsuse, J. I., 18
Knopoff, K., 30
KnorrCetina, K., 3, 15, 19,
    26, 27, 44, 79
Knowledge, status of, 18
Knowledge proposal, 18
Kram, K. E., 21, 38–39
Kramer, R. J., 41
Kunda, G., 16, 73

Lammers, C. J., 34
Lamott, A., 12, 114
Langer, S., 16, 92
Langley, A., 29
Langton, J., 36
Latour, B., 3, 18, 79
Law, J., 48
Lewontin, R., 33
Lilius, J., 29
Literary elements
    figurative language, 19
    metaphor (*See* Metaphor)
    qualifier, 20–21, 28–29, 43
Llewellyn, S., 22
Locke, K., 10, 15, 16, 17, 19, 20,
    26, 27, 31, 32, 33, 38, 76, 77, 82
    (tab), 90, 116
Lord, M. D., 16
Lyne, J., 15

"Maintaining Norms About Expressed
    Emotions: The Case of Bill
    Collectors" (Sutton), 87
Maitlis, S., 50
Majchrzak, A., 16
Managerial discourse,
    101–102, 107–108
March, J., 19, 33
Marcus, G., 19
Marcus, G. E., 1
Markus, L. M., 16
Martin, J., 30, 74

McCloskey, D. N., 3–4, 16, 19, 64, 69
McDaniel, R., 16, 28–29
McKinley, W., 15, 16
Meaning-making process, iterative,
    81, 108, 115
Mentors, 21, 38–39
Metaphor
    characterization, 22
    conversation, 16–17
    football game, 21
    story, 5–6
    time famine, 85, 97, 98
    two-way window, 22
Methodology section, 51–52
Miller, W. L., 16, 28–29
Miner, A. S., 38
Minimally expressive writing, 10–11
Momer, K., 79
Mone, M., 16
Mone, M. A., 15
Monologic view of text, 19
Moon, G., 15
Moorman, C., 38
Morse, J. M., 16, 47
Mottier, V., 64
Mulkay, M., 19
Multivocal nature, of data, 26,
    89–90, 113–114
Mumby, D., 19

Nadkarni, S., 73
Najjar, H., 26, 27, 44
Narayanan, V., 73
Nelson, K., 73
Ng, W., 35, 50
Noncoherence, 36–37
Nonfiction short story, journal
    article as, 25
Nonornamental prose, 10–11

Objective reality, 14
Ofori-Dankwa, J., 15
Okhuysen, G. A., 37
"The Organizational and
    Interorganizational Development
    of Disasters" (Turner), 57–58
Organizational studies, 84, 95

Organizations, issues faced by
    bankruptcy, 22
    board functioning, 35, 40–41, 49–51
    change, 98–99, 102–107
    computerization, 65–66, 70–71
    control/performance, 29, 37
    decision making, 16, 43–44, 50
    disaster, 100
    environments, 6, 14, 57–58,
        91, 101–102
    homelessness, 55, 89
    identity, 21, 92, 94–96, 105
    incomplete problematization, 38–39
    managerial discourse, 101–102,
        107–108
    mentors, 21, 38–39
    physician-patient relations,
        32–33, 44–45
    social workers, 53–54
    storytelling, 43, 87, 88–89
    time use, 96–98
Organizations (March & Simon), 19, 33
Orlikowski, W. J., 16, 46, 47, 82 (tab),
    84, 102–105, 108

Paradis, J., 3, 9
Partisanship, 41–42
Passive voice, extensive use of, 11
Patton, M. Q., 72
Pentland, B. T., 51–52
Perlow, L. A., 37, 82 (tab), 84, 85,
    86, 96–98
Personal pronouns, 11, 66–67, 74–75
Persuasive writing, 17–20
Physician-patient relations, 32–33, 44–45
Pinder, C., 11, 19
Pineault, M., 29
Poetic language, 3
Pooler, C., 16, 47
Prasad, P., 39–40
Pratt, M. G., 47, 83 (tab), 85, 88,
    92, 94–96, 109
"Presenting Structural Innovation in an
    Institutional Environment:
    Hospitals' Use of Impression
    Management" (Arndt & Bigelow),
    91, 101–102

Prior, P., 3
Problem domains, 15
Problematizing the literature
    inadequate, 39–41, 42–43
    incommensurate, 41–44
    incomplete, 38–39
Process-based view of events, 5–6, 25
Progressive coherence, 34–36,
    40–41, 45–46
Pronouns, personal, 11, 66–67, 74–75
Putnam, L., 19

Qualifiers, 20–21, 28–29, 43
Quotation marks, 69

Rabinow, P., 1, 3, 64
Ranft, A. L., 16
Rankin, E., 16
Rao, H. V., 82 (tab), 90–91, 99, 108
Rausch, R., 79
Reader-receptive characters, 63
Reality, shaped by experience, 14
Reay, T., 15–16, 33, 52
Reflected glory, 76
Related works. *See* Intertextual
    coherence
Repenning, N. P., 37
Research intersections between
    progress, 32–33
Research network, 15
Research report, as human
    construction, 17
Resolution, for theoretical story, 25–26
"Resources in Emerging Structures and
    Processes of Change" (Feldman),
    98–99, 105–106
Review process
    reviewer *vs.* editor focus, 87, 91–100
    source materials for analyzation,
        105–107
    substantial changes request, 109–110
    See also Re-writing
Reviewer/editor, substantial changes
    requested by, 109–110
Re-writing, 81–111
    articulated theorized storylines,
        91–108

author and reviewer
    suggestions, 100–108
completing intertextual field,
    96, 99, 100
data-theory coupling,
    tightening, 55–57
during journal review process, 86–91
engaging/re-writing field story, 87–91
positioning in different contextual
    field, 99–100
prior to journal review, 83–86
profiled articles for, 82 (tab)–83 (tab)
reflection on, 108–110
refocusing storyline, 108
theoretical significance/positioning
    data, 92
title change, 93 (tab)–94 (tab)
Rhetoric, 18–20
Richardson, L., 13, 14, 15
Riley, P., 37
Rockmann, K., 47, 83 (tab), 85, 88
"The Role of Organizational
    Identity and Image"
    (Dutton & Dukerich), 55
Rorty, R., 1, 10–11, 18
Ross, J., 69
Rousseau, D., 87

Sahay, S., 47, 70–71, 82 (tab), 84, 109
Sandberg, J., 27
Sarker, S., 47
Schein, E., 47
Schultz, U., 67–68
Scientific demonstration, disembodied
    voice of, 10–11
Scientific writing
    a-rhetorical view of, 19
    as constructed, 14
    as human performance, 13
    inaccessibility of, 11–12
    See also Style/practice, of
        professional writing
Scientist style, in academic writing,
    11–12, 19
Selzer, J., 4, 18
Sharing writing, 115
Significance factor, 27–31

Simon, H., 19, 33
Smircich, L., 19
Smith, A. D., 115
"Social Poetics as Management
    Inquiry: A Dialogical Approach"
    (Cunliffe), 107–108
Social workers, 53–54
Sociology, new research
    traditions in, 19
Socrates, 61–62
Specialty audience, 15
Spector, M., 18
Stange, K. C., 16, 28–29
Staw, B. M., 69
"Stories of the Storytelling
    Organization: A Postmodern
    Analysis of Disney as 'Tamara-
    Land'" (Boje), 87, 88–89
Story metaphor, 5–6
Storyline, theorized. See Theorized
    storyline, crafting
Storyteller, 61–79
    as individual human character,
        64, 66–68
    field knowledgeable, 76–78
    relation to studied, 70–71
    technical competence, 72–75
    as institutional scientist, 64–66
    atypical, 75
    authorial (non)-presence, 65–66
    data as evidence for, 69, 70
    field knowledgeable, 76–78
    first person, 66–67
    objectivity, 69–70
    reader-receptive characters, 63–64
    technical competence, 72–74
    third person, 66
Socrates, 61–62
Strauss, A., 64, 76
Style/practice, of professional
    writing, 9–24
    audience, 14–17, 18, 62
    components of writing task, 23–24
    constructed reality, 14
    nonornamental prose, 10–11
    passive voice, 11
    persuasive discourse, 17–23

reviews of final work
    uncomplicated transitions, 54–55
    windowpane model of language,
        10, 13, 17, 68
Sullivan, W. M., 1, 3, 64
Sutton, R. I., 16, 34, 82 (tab), 87, 88, 89
Swales, J., 26, 27, 44
Synthesized coherence, 33–34, 40

Taylor, R. N., 9
"The Textual Approach: Risk and
    Blame in Disaster Sensemaking"
    (Gephart), 93
Theorized story, 5, 6
    vs. field-based story, 57–60
    vs. literature-based story, 26
Theorized storyline, crafting, 25–46
    complication/development/resolution,
        25–26
    literature review, 31–37
    noncoherence approach, 36–37
    progressive coherence approach,
        34–36, 40–41, 45–46
    synthesized coherence approach,
        33–34, 40
    problematizing literature, 37–44
    research gap, 44–46
    study significance, 27–31
    See also Theorized storyline,
        developing
Theorized storyline, developing
    complication, introducing, 57–60
    data-theory coupling, 52–57
    dramatic moments, 22–23
    field/theory complications, 57–60
    finding theoretical connection,
        100, 106–107
    introductory paragraph, 48–51
    methodology section, 51–52
    transporting reader into field, 48
    vs. field-based stories, 57–60
    See also Intertextual coherence;
        Theorized storyline, crafting
Thomas, D. A., 41
Time famine metaphor, 85, 97, 98
"The Time Famine: Toward a Sociology
    of Work" (Perlow), 96

Transitions, in writing, 54–55
Trauth, E. M., 47
Turner, B. A., 47, 57–59
Turner, P. K., 67
Two-way window metaphor, 22

Van Maanen, J., 3, 13, 14, 19,
    47, 65, 69, 75, 77
Vaughan, D., 47
Verbatim data, 56–57, 69

Walsham, G., 70–71, 82 (tab), 84, 109
Warren, R. P., 10
Watson, T. J., 13, 19
Weick, K. E., 6, 47
Weighting data, 70
Whiteman, G., 77
Williams, R., 48

Windowpane model of language,
    10, 13, 17, 68
Winsor, D., 4, 18
Wolcott, H., 3
Woolgar, S., 3, 18, 79
Worline, M., 29
Writing
    about writing, 2–4
    as social process, 115
    Kantian perspective on, 10–11
    silence on, 115
Writing process
    demystifying, 20, 113, 116
    reading, 115–116
    sharing, 115
    writing/re-writing, 114–115

Yan, A., 36

ABOUT THE AUTHORS

Karen Golden-Biddle is Professor, Health System Management and Change in the Strategic Management and Organization department, University of Alberta School of Business. She earned her Ph.D. in management and policy studies from Case Western Reserve University. Her research examines the processes and symbolics of organizational change, and the use of qualitative data in theorizing organizational phenomena. She has published in journals such as *Academy of Management Journal, Journal of Health Services Research and Policy, Journal of Management Studies,* and *Organization Science.* She was Principal Investigator on a five-year investigation (2000–2005) of organizational change in the Canadian health care system funded by the Canadian Health Services Research Foundation and the Alberta Heritage Foundation for Medical Research. This field research involved a team of interdisciplinary researchers from multiple universities working in collaboration with practicing managers. She has also served on numerous editorial boards and was recently elected to the Board of Governors of the Academy of Management.

Karen Locke is W. Brooks George Professor of Business Administration at the College of William and Mary's school of business, where she is a member of the management area. She joined the faculty there in 1989 after earning her Ph.D. in organizational behavior from Case Western Reserve University. Her work focuses on developing a sociology of knowledge in organizational studies with an emphasis on the production of scientific texts and on the use of qualitative research for the investigation of organizational phenomena. She has published in journals such as *Academy of Management Journal, Organization Science,* and *Studies in Organization, Culture and Society,* and has authored *Grounded Theory in Management Research.* Her current work continues her interest in the processes of qualitative researching and focuses on exploring and explicating their creative and imaginative dimensions. She also serves as an associate action editor for *Organizational Research Methods* and as a member of the editorial board of *Academy of Management Journal.*